Boulevard Comedies

Boulevard Comedies

֍

FREE ADAPTATIONS OF
BECQUE, FEYDEAU AND MOLIÈRE

by Charles Marowitz

Great Translations Series

SK
A Smith and Kraus Book

A Smith and Kraus Book
Published by Smith and Kraus, Inc.
PO Box 127, Lyme, NH 03768
www.SmithKraus.com

Copyright ©2000 Charles Marowitz
All rights reserved
Manufactured in the United States of America

Cover and Text Design by Julia Hill Gignoux, Freedom Hill Design

First Edition: Feb 2000
10 9 8 7 6 5 4 3 2 1

CAUTION: Professionals and amateurs are hereby warned that the plays represented in this book are subject to a royalty. They are fully protected under the copyright laws of the United States of America, and of all countries covered by the International Copyright Union (including the Dominion of Canada and the rest of the British Commonwealth), and of all countries covered by the Pan-American Copyright Convention and the Universal Copyright Convention, and of all countries with which the United States has reciprocal copyright relations. All rights, including professional, amateur, motion picture, recitation, lecturing, public reading, radio broadcasting, television, video or sound taping, all other forms of mechanical or electronic reproductions such as CD-ROM and CD-I, information storage and retrieval systems and photocopying, and the rights of translation into foreign languages, are strictly reserved. Particular emphasis is laid upon the question of public readings, permission for which must be secured from the Author's agent in writing. All inquiries concerning rights, other than amateur rights, should be addressed to Jane Windsor, 3058 Sequit Drive, Malibu, CA. 90265, Fx. 310-456-8170.

The Library of Congress Cataloging-In-Publication Data
Marowitz, Charles.
Boulevard comedies: free adaptations of Becque, Feydeau, and Molière / by Charles Marowitz. —1st ed.
p. cm. — (Great translations series)
Contents: Introduction / by Charles marowitz — Georges Feydeau's Stark naked — Henry Becque's La Parisienne — Quack / by Charles Marowitz; music by Michael Valenti; based on Molière's The physician in spite of himself.
ISBN 1-57525-210-4
1. French drama (Comedy) — Adaptations.
I. Feydeau, Georges, 1862–1921. Mais n'te promene donc pas toute nue.
II. Becque, Henry, 1837–1899. Parisienne.
III. Molière, 1622–1673. Médecin malgré lui.
IV. Title. V. Great translations for actors series.

PS3563.A68 B68 1999
812'.54—dc21   99-052455

Contents

Introduction *You Take the High Road; I'll Take the Low Road* by Charles Marowitz — vii

Georges Feydeau's *Stark Naked* — 1
"Mais N'te Promene Donc Pas Toute Nue"

Henry Becque's *La Parisienne* — 35

Quack by Charles Marowitz, Music by Michael Valenti — 77
Based on Molière's *The Physician in Spite of Himself*

Introduction

YOU TAKE THE HIGH ROAD; I'LL TAKE THE LOW ROAD

by Charles Marowitz

The "Boulevard," like Broadway, is more a state of mind than a geographical location. It is theatre created to satisfy the more immediate needs of the majority audience; the audience which prefers to be amused rather than challenged, gratified rather than provoked, reassured rather than disturbed.

These are entertainments consciously manufactured for "the tired business man" and the family outing. Boulevard Theatre has always inhabited a sphere several degrees below that of the Serious Drama. Its nearest kin are the Cabaret and the Music Hall and, although it often believes itself to be superior to those vulgar diversions, it is actually bred in the same gene pool.

Boulevard Theatre is the equivalent of a good meal and a bubbly bottle of champagne. It is, in Bertolt Brecht's disparaging phrase, "culinary theatre" and shamelessly so. It feeds on amoristic peccadilloes, mistaken identities, interrupted trysts, deflated pomposities, and utilizes both physical and philosophical pratfalls. About a century ago, the proponents of Serious Theatre saw it as "the enemy" and it was what inspired them to *èpater le bourgeois*. Without the smug complacency of the *boulevardiers* who happily supported such diversions, there would never have been either an Epic Theatre or a Theater of Cruelty. In a world that was constantly cultivating its palate for more and more rarefied artistic fare, it was the quintessence of junk food.

But then, as now, junk food served a purpose and there is a *frisson* to be had from a hamburger and a milk shake that defies the delicate pleasures derived from haute cuisine. Paradoxically, the greatest artists tended to indulge in helpings of junk food on the sly. Brecht adored the smoky cabarets where troubadours sang satirical little ditties or maudlin ballads about soured romance.

Antonin Artaud adored the Marx Brothers and found in them the seeds of a liberating surrealism. George Jean Nathan, the drumbeater for Eugene O'Neill and the new European drama, was an habitué of burlesque shows and doted on the Ziegfeld Follies. And how many great American and European novelists admit to an insatiable appetite for detective pulp-fiction, thrillers and sci-fi adventures?

∽

From the middle of the 19th century through to the end of the Belle Epoch, the Boulevard flourished in France and there were countless numbers of writers feeding the frenzy. Many were hacks; others were seminal artists who markedly influenced the shape and feel of the modern theatre.

Henry Becque (1837–1899) coasted on to the French stage on the wave of Naturalism which had been started by writers such as Ibsen and Hauptman. He was a kindred spirit with Zola and, while the Boulevard Theatre was still in the grip of romanticism, had the temerity to create "slices of life" which showed the French public their true nature. Becque was an unrepentant "disturber of the peace" who exposed the French to aspects of their society which they preferred to ignore.

Long before Antonin Artaud came on the scene, Becque was espousing the cause of "a cruel theatre" which would present life's grubbier realities. He made many enemies, but fortunately had enough friends to get his difficult plays mounted in theatres like the Comedie Francaise. *La Parisienne,* although a comedy, took a cold, hard look at French immorality and didn't recoil from what it saw. Becque lifted the veil of romance from illicit love and, in the process, made many husbands and wives squirm in their seats. After its production in 1885, the conventional naughty "triangle play" which had regaled French audiences for decades was done forever.

Georges Feydeau (1862–1921) the creator of some of France's wildest farces, was himself surprisingly non-Feydeauesque. "I never laugh in the theatre," he confessed, "and I seldom laugh in private life. I am taciturn and somewhat unsociable." Contrary to all the rules of playwriting as taught in workshops and colleges throughout America, Feydeau never worked from an outline and never produced a "first draft." "My plays are entirely improvised," he said, "the whole and the parts, the design and the shape all fall into place when I am writing."

His target was always the same: the foibles and hypocrisies of the bourgeoisie. Behind every social facade, Feydeau believed, there was greed, lust, stupidity and delusion; the delusion being that society could impose civilized behavior on a primitive species and create rules to which they would faithfully abide. Long before Freud, Feydeau knew that the super-ego was merely the mask that the id wore to camouflage its more ravenous drives. Unlike his tamer contemporaries (Victorien Sardou, Eugene Labiche, Maurice Donnay), there is a barbaric strain to Feydeau's comedy which brings to mind the dangerous ferocity of untamed children at play.

To the French, adultery was both irresistible and hilarious. (How different a reaction from puritanical Americans who would impeach a President for having "a little on the side" and risk throwing the whole nation into turmoil because a philandering husband had strayed from his marital vows.) Becque's *La Parisienne* is, in one sense, a typical comedy-of-cuckoldry, but in another, a study on the consequences of suppressing natural instincts. Like all good comedy, it is played on the verge of marital tragedy. If one removes the deliberate farcicality of many of these plays and cold-bloodedly examines their social imbroglios, they become chilling indictments of domesticity.

Feydeau's *Stark Naked*, like almost all of French Boulevard Comedy, owes a clear debt to Molière. Without the naive wife and the controlling husband, the philistine onlooker and the horny intruder, farce could not exist and it was Moliere who created the boilerplates for all these types. In *Mais N'te Promene Donc Pas Toute Nue*, Feydeau examines the terrors associated with the human body and how they threaten the *sang-froid* of certain up-tight pillars of Respectability. Again, a modern parallel presents itself in the way that, not too long ago, certain members of the American congress were outraged by the revelations of Clinton's sexual liaison with a White House intern. Instead of openly expressing disgust, their enflamed morality took refuge behind moral platitudes, and behavior which is commonplace, universal and inescapably natural, was construed as violating some holy commandment from above. Feydeau would have loathed the Clinton-Lewinsky scandal for appropriating into the political arena salacious material which is essentially the purview of the Boulevard Theatre.

Molière, being one century removed, may seem to be odd man out in this collection, but in one sense, it was Molière who created the Boulevard mentality. Examining his oeuvre, one tends to wonder: did Molière *invent* infidelity, cuckoldry and the triangular relationship? Could it be because of *him* that Frenchmen have mistresses, are jealous, horny, tortured and prone to intrigue and deceptions? Probably not. And yet I can think of no classic playwright, Shakespeare and Chekhov included, whose work has left so impermeable a mark on the social and sexual habits of a nation. Swedes are not Strindbergian nor Norwegians Ibsenic, but the French, in their social posture and sexual mores, are unmistakably fashioned in the mold of Molière.

Eighteenth century playwrights stole liberally from Molière's works and "englished" them in numerous "adaptations." He is also the progenitor of the saucy vaudeville sketch and the burlesque blackout. (Could Smith and Dale have created "Dr. Kronkheit" without him?) His situations reoccur in Neil Simon and Alan Ayckbourn. His critique of religion is, if anything, more pertinent today than it was four hundred years ago. Despite the royal patronage and the cosying-up to French nobility, he was a man who played shamelessly to the groundlings, and they loved him for it.

In an era in which HMOs tend to stand for Horrible Medical Outrages, *The Physician in Spite of Himself* is a harsh satire which turns the scalpel on those that usually wield it. The essence of its comedy — the alacrity with which the gullible are taken in by bogus professional practitioners—is, in our era of New Age remedies and Alternative Medicine, a highly relevant cautionary tale. It is, essentially, an extended vaudeville sketch and in its original form already resembles a kind of libretto; a short, spare "book" asking for the amplification of song and dance — which is what I and composer Michael Valenti have given it. The diction has changed considerably, but the attitudes and ideas expressed are quintessentially those of Jean Baptiste Poquelin.

A word about the term "adaptation" as it applies to all of these works.

My aim has been to take the plays and run freely with them—not always in the directions originally staked out by their authors. I would hope the spirit of these writers has been lovingly preserved, even when the letter has gone through some radical transformations. Of course, this is always the defense of the modern translator—that he is re-tooling old works for a modern sensibility. But in the case of Becque, Feydeau and Molière I find the "modern sensibility" is organically rooted in the original material. Changes of idiom are not *fundamental* changes. If they were, the Germans could never lay claim to Shakespeare as they do, or the English to Ibsen.

I would hope that whatever opprobrium is attached to the idea of "Boulevard Theatre," it will be somewhat mitigated (it cannot be removed) by these three plays. When one comes right down to it, Boulevard Theatre is the midway of mass entertainment. It is populated not only by hacks and calculating scribblers, but also by artists such as Eugene Brieux, Eugene Scribe, Arthur Schnitzler, Ferenc Molnar, Johan Strauss Jr., Jacques Offenbach, Franz Lehar, Rudolph Friml, Victor Herbert, Rodgers and Hart, Kern and Hammerstein, Cole Porter, Irving Berlin and Andrew Lloyd Webber. It is populist in the very best sense of the word in that it reaches out to the variegated masses, requesting the pleasure of their company and in return provides easily obtained emotional satisfaction.

Georges Feydeau's

STARK NAKED

"Mais N'te Promene Donc Pas Toute Nue!"

Translated and Freely Adapted
by Charles Marowitz

Cast of Characters

VENTROUX, a politician
CLARISSE, his wife
VICTOR, their man-servant
HIMMELFAAHRT, a local dignitary
ROMAIN DE JAIVAL, a journalist

SCENE: The VENTROUX's living room. A comfortable, bourgeois home in Paris. Doors to bedroom, study and a vestibule which leads outdoors. A prominent window upstage which contains a lace blind which has slid off its railing and trails on the floor.

As the Curtain rises, VICTOR is discovered on a stepladder repairing the cords on the window-blind. Offstage, in CLARISSE'S room, voices are barely audible, but those of VENTROUX and his son AUGUSTE predominate.

VENTROUX's VOICE: *(Offstage.)* What are you saying, CLARISSE? *(A muffled reply from CLARISSE.)* I don't know, as soon as the Session ends we'll head out to Deauville.
VOICE OF VENTROUX's SON: *(Offstage. Excitedly.)* Oh yes, daddy—Deauville, Deauville.
VENTROUX's VOICE: *(Concerned.)* Hold off, there Clarisse. Just hold off.
CLARISSE's VOICE: Just a minute—till I change.
VENTROUX's VOICE: *(Growing hysterical.)* Clarisse? What are you doing? Are you mad?
CLARISSE's VOICE: What're you saying?
VENTROUX's VOICE: For God's sake woman! Your son is standing right there!
CLARISSE's VOICE: I'll only be a minute.
VENTROUX's VOICE: Stop, stop at once! We can see you plain as day. Have you gone off your head!?
CLARISSE's VOICE: Oh, what a bore you are! Making such a fuss!
VENTROUX's VOICE: I'm leaving. I will not be witness to such…such… Auguste, out! Out of the room!!!
   (A door is heard slamming loudly. Throughout this exchange, VICTOR, immobilized on the stepladder, has been listening to the racket.)
VENTROUX'S VOICE: Out, I say! At once! IMMEDIATELY!
VOICE OF VENTROUX's SON: I'm going, papa.—What are you screaming about!?
   (VENTROUX enters slamming the door shut behind him. He is in a pinstriped suit; very formal and conservative.)
VENTROUX: What gross indecency! *(Suddenly spies VICTOR.)* What the hell are you doing up there?
VICTOR: *(Beat, looks about.)* Madame told me to fix the blinds.
VENTROUX: Can't you see I'm having a private conversation with my wife? Have you no tact?

STARK NAKED • 3

VICTOR: *(Looking at window.)* It don't need tacks—just some string and a little wire.

VENTROUX: Stop being stupid. You were listening at the door.

VICTOR: *(Looking about.)* But I'm at the window.

VENTROUX: Peeking through the keyhole.

VICTOR: There's no keyhole in the window.

VENTROUX: There is at the door.

VICTOR: But I'm at the window.

VENTROUX: Don't think you can get round me with logic, Victor. Come down off the ladder and get the hell out of here!

VICTOR: But Madame said…

VENTROUX: Damn Madame! And damn you as well. — Out, I say! *(He hustles VICTOR down from the stepladder leaving the blind to dangle and the window fully exposed.)* And take that stupid stepladder with you!

VICTOR: As you say, sir.

(Attempting to leave, he picks up the stepladder and swings it horizontally, just missing VENTROUX. Then as he bends down for his tool kit and turns to go, the ladder swings round to the other side, just missing VENTROUX again.)

VENTROUX: *(Exasperated at his slow exit.)* Are you through!?

VICTOR: *(Misunderstanding.)* Not really; I've still got the blind to do and …

VENTROUX: *(Losing it.)* Get out, get out, get out!

(VICTOR scrambles out but gets wedged in the doorway because of the ladder. He tries unsuccessfully to close it up. VENTROUX, boiling with rage, closes it for him, getting his finger caught in the process, and finally bundles him out of the room.)

(CLARISSE emerges from the bedroom. She is wearing a see-through nightie which leaves nothing to the imagination, high-heeled shoes and a hat.)

CLARISSE: Now, would you kindly tell me what all the fuss is about?

VENTROUX: *(To VICTOR offstage.)* And watch out for my flowerpots with that damn ladder, do you hear? *(Turns to CLARISSE but doesn't quite take her in, turns back to the door.)* That fellow is a retard, if you ask me, there's something wrong with his…*(Stops short; the image of his wife registers; he turns back quickly and takes in his wife's appearance.)* No, no! Don't tell me you're going to walk around like that?!—And with that hat?

CLARISSE: What *has* got into you? And this is a perfectly good hat. It cost me fifty francs.

VENTROUX: I'm not talking about your hat. I'm talking about…about…Oh God, oh God!
CLARISSE: Are you ill. What *is* the matter?
VENTROUX: The matter?!—What is the matter?!
CLARISSE: There's nothing the matter with me.—What have I done now?
VENTROUX: *(Heavily ironic.)* Done? Nothing, nothing at all. What could you possibly have done?
CLARISSE: Then what are you going on about…?
VENTROUX: If you have no idea of the effects of your actions…of the consequences of your atrocious behavior—of your—
CLARISSE: Will you stop talking and just talk!
VENTROUX: *(After a short take on her last.)* You think it's decent do you, to change into your nightie with your son standing right there in front of you!?
CLARISSE: Is all this about that?—My God, you'd think I'd plunged a knife into somebody's heart.
VENTROUX: You might just as well have done.—You think that is normal behavior, do you?
CLARISSE: *(Brushing it off.)* Stop being ridiculous! Auguste is just a baby. He doesn't notice a thing—and even if he did, I am his mother, after all.
VENTROUX: A baby!?
CLARISSE: He's only twelve.
VENTROUX: It's not done, Clarisse. In the best homes, it simply isn't done.—And he's not twelve he's thirteen.
CLARISSE: He's twelve!
VENTROUX: He's thirteen. His birthday was three days ago.
CLARISSE: So twelve and three days!
VENTROUX: He's *thirteen*, Clarisse. He's a man. A boy is a man when he gets to be thirteen. And even if he's twelve, he's more a man than a boy. A "boy" is three or four or maybe five.
CLARISSE: *(The logician.)* Well, he's *been* three-and-four-and-five.
VENTROUX: I know damn well he's *been* three-and-four-and-five, but now he's thirteen!
CLARISSE: He doesn't even know what a woman is yet?
VENTROUX: And I'd like to keep it that way! It's not for you to introduce him to the subject. That'll be my job, if it's anyone's and I'm not sure it *is* anyone's! What is this maniacal obsession you have with going about naked?
CLARISSE: Naked? Don't be absurd. You can see I'm wearing a nightie.
VENTROUX: *The whole neighborhood can see you're wearing a nightie!!!* It might as well be made of cellophane or air molecules.

CLARISSE: Oh, now I see. You would prefer to see me walking around in a cotton chemise, or buckram perhaps. Or why not wool?

VENTROUX: What are you talking about?

CLARISSE: I'm talking about "fashion," Julien. A subject about which you appear to be entirely ignorant. Women of my station in life, a Minister's wife living in one of the most select neighborhoods in Paris, has negligees of lace or silk. But no, you'd have me lounging around in alpaca or perhaps raccoon skin.

VENTROUX: *(Truly confused.)* What exactly are we talking about?

CLARISSE: What would people say to that?

VENTROUX: What people?

CLARISSE: The people who'd see me lounging around in a thick, bulky nightgown?

VENTROUX: Why should *anyone* see you lounging around in any kind of nightgown?

CLARISSE: My point exactly!

VENTROUX: And what point is that?

CLARISSE: Don't ask me, you started all this.

VENTROUX: Just stop it, Clarisse. You're turning things topsy-turvy as you always do. I'm not asking you to wear nightgowns made of alpaca or raccoon or asbestos or anything else. I am simply asking that when your son is in the room you have the basic decency not to strip down to the buff in front of him.

CLARISSE: Which is exactly what I did.

VENTROUX: What you did?

CLARISSE: Since I know how squeamish you are and you were both in there together, I went into the bathroom to get changed.

VENTROUX: To get changed into *that?*

CLARISSE: Exactly. And it was only after I'd changed into my nightie that I came out.

VENTROUX: Like *that?*

CLARISSE: Precisely, so you see how unfair you're being.

VENTROUX: *(Eyes upraised.)* God give me strength.

CLARISSE: *(Under her breath.)* I hope He does! You can certainly use some—especially in bed.

VENTROUX: *(Sensing an insult.)* What did you say?

CLARISSE: *(Aside.)* Let's not open that can of worms.

VENTROUX: *(His manhood offended.)* What did you call it?

CLARISSE: Let's stick to one subject at a time, shall we?

VENTROUX: *(At boiling point.)* Why do you need to change into your nightie at four-thirty in the afternoon anyway?

CLARISSE: You ask that! After suffocating at the Doumier girl's wedding for nearly four hours. The sweat was pouring off me in buckets. And why was I there, answer me that? Do I even know that Doumier girl?—Or *want* to know her? No!—Her father is some big wig in your Ministry and so I had to sacrifice myself to please you. Swim about in that hot-box for *your* sake! — And this is the thanks I get.

VENTROUX: This has nothing to do with being thankful.

CLARISSE: Oh I know very well, I owe everything to you and must expect nothing in return. If I held my breath waiting to receive a "thank you" from you, I'd have expired long ago. Nevertheless, when I am drenched in sweat, soaked to the skin, smelling like an abattoir and need to change into something more comfortable, I would have thought you'd allow me that, at the very least.

VENTROUX: Well, I agree, you do have a point there.

CLARISSE: He agrees. How mag*nam*inous.

VENTROUX: *(Correcting her.)* "Magnanimous."

CLARISSE: That's what I said.

VENTROUX: You said—

CLARISSE: Oh it's all right for you drinking wine in the shade of the patio with your political cronies, but I was inside where it was at least ninety-six degrees latitude.

VENTROUX: *(Beat.)* Latitude?

CLARISSE: Exactly. Ninety-six degrees at the very least.

VENTROUX: What is "latitude"; what do you mean "latitude"?

CLARISSE: You don't know what latitude means? You, a Minister of State, a man who is at the very top of our government, and you don't know what latitude means!? That's really pathetic, Julien. Really. *(Then turning with a blast of condescension.)* Latitude, darling, is what you have on the thermometer.

VENTROUX: I see. Don't know how I could have missed that.

CLARISSE: First the mind goes, then the body, isn't that what they say.

VENTROUX: I'll take *your* word for that.

CLARISSE: No need to; read Balzac, read Anatole France, it's all there.

VENTROUX: Have *you* read Balzac and Anatole France?

CLARISSE: Why would I waste my time reading books? *I'm* not a Minister. Although God knows, if *you're* one, I could be President of the Republic.

VENTROUX: You may have a point there.

CLARISSE: Two in one day. I *am* improving.—When I think that I have to stay cooped up here in Paris in ninety-six degrees latitude, all because of you being

STARK NAKED • 7

in the Ministry and us having to wait for the Session to end…as if the Parliament would fall apart if you weren't there.
VENTROUX: Whether it would fall apart or not is not the point. When one accepts a position of responsibility, one has to fulfill one's duty. What if every Minister left town insisting his services were not required? Why the whole government would shut down.
CLARISSE: I don't see that that would make a blind bit of difference. The country seems to run quite well when they *are* shut down. And life is very much more pleasant.
VENTROUX: We were not elected to make life more pleasant. If we wanted that, we wouldn't need politicians at all.
CLARISSE: Exactly.
VENTROUX: What do you mean, "exactly"?
CLARISSE: What you just said.
VENTROUX: What did I just say?
CLARISSE: Well if you weren't listening, I'm not going back over the whole business.
VENTROUX: You're doing it again. Running me around in circles.
CLARISSE: Don't be silly, Julien. A man in your weakened condition shouldn't *dream* of running around in circles. Why even trudging up the stairs would pose a major health hazard.
VENTROUX: *(Fuming.)* I was not talking about politics.
CLARISSE: Neither was I.—Really, you're impossible today.
VENTROUX: The question is not about the Ministry or leaving Paris; the question is why do you find it necessary to walk around without clothes on? One thing has nothing to do with the other.
CLARISSE: I beg to differ. Because of your Ministry, we are still here in Paris where it is ninety-six degrees latitude…
VENTROUX: Oh, not again.
CLARISSE: Because when it is ninety-six degrees latitude, I perspire, and when I perspire, I feel the need to change my clothes, and when I feel the need to get out of my clothes, you feel the need to hit the roof.
VENTROUX: I am not hitting the roof because you changed your clothes, but because you changed your clothes and are parading in front of your son in a transparent nightie with all your personal and private…appendages…hanging out.
CLARISSE: I can't see that.
VENTROUX: Everyone else can!
CLARISSE: It's not my fault my nightie is transparent.

VENTROUX: No, but it *is* your fault if you walk into the living room wearing it.

CLARISSE: Well that takes the cake! I no longer have the right to walk into my own living room!

VENTROUX: I didn't say that. Don't put words into my mouth.

CLARISSE: Where would you like me to get undressed? In the kitchen? Up in the attic perhaps? In front of the servants? —Oh, that would get you going I'm sure.

VENTROUX: You're using a specious argument.

CLARISSE: You're the one that's 'suspecious', not me.

VENTROUX: *(Boiling.)* There's no such word as "suspecious."

CLARISSE: Then stop using it, for God's sake!!! And stop these stupid accusations. It was my room. You had no business being in there. Did I invite you in? —No, you just *barged* in. If my appearance bothered you, you should have left.

VENTROUX: You're not being logical!

CLARISSE: I'm a woman; I don't have to be.—Making such a fuss because I walked in to put on my nightie. *(Screeching at him.)* What was I to do? The nightie was *in my room!*

VENTROUX: You could have asked me to get it for you.

CLARISSE: Then *you* would have seen me naked.

VENTROUX: So what?—I'm your husband!

CLARISSE: And Auguste's my son!

VENTROUX: *(Pulling his hair, near tears.)* Impossible, impossible!—So for you it's all the same.

CLARISSE: It's not the same at all!

VENTROUX: *(Believing sense has finally broken through.)* At last.

CLARISSE: He's closer.

VENTROUX: What?

CLARISSE: Just think about it—logically. Who are you? A stranger. Oh, you're my husband of course, but that's just a social convention. When I married you—and I can't even remember why exactly—

VENTROUX: Thanks very much.

CLARISSE: *(Pushing on.)*...I hardly knew you. Then "Poof"—in the space of a day, and all because some pompous preacher waving a prayer book said "Yes, *you're* allowed see me naked. — Well, I call *that* indecent.

VENTROUX: *(Reboiling.)* You do, ey, —"indecent"?

CLARISSE: But as for my son, he's my own flesh and blood. Well then, if the flesh-of-my-flesh sees my flesh, there's nothing indecent about that.—It's sheer prejudice, nothing more.

STARK NAKED • 9

VENTROUX: Prejudice, you say, prejudice. *(Screeching.)* But prejudice is everything—everything!

CLARISSE: *(Haughtily.)* For the petite-bourgeois perhaps, but thank God, I'm above all that.

VENTROUX: *(Collapsing onto the couch with exasperation, muttering to himself.)* She's above all that. How nice. How convenient. Above it all.

CLARISSE: *(Feeling she is conquering, keeps up the attack.)* The boy has seen me get dressed and undressed at least twenty thousand times since he was born, and you never said a word!

VENTROUX: *(Muttering to himself.)* I never said a word—I never said a word. *(Forcing himself out of his manic shell.)* But it had to stop sometime, didn't it?

CLARISSE: *(Exasperatingly calm.)* Of course it did; no one denies that.

VENTROUX: *(Still blabbering madly.)* Well then…well then…well then?

CLARISSE: Fine, well then—when?

VENTROUX: When?—What when?

CLARISSE: When? What day? What time?

VENTROUX: *(Parroting her.)* When? What day?? What time???

CLARISSE: There has to be a day—a time. Why particularly today? Why not yesterday? Why not tomorrow?—So I ask you: When? What day? What time?

VENTROUX: *(Mocking her.)* When—what day—what time?—How should I know? You expect me to provide you with a precise time?

CLARISSE: Ah, so you can't *be* precise. Oh, that's priceless. So you want me—a woman—who by definition is less intelligent than you—(*your* definition that is)—you want *me* to do something that you admit you cannot!

VENTROUX: *(Suffering.)* My God, I feel as if my brains have been thrown into a pot of boiling water and are now leaking out through my ears.

CLARISSE: Shall I get you a towel?

VENTROUX: *(Exploding.)* I don't want a towel. I want sanity.

CLARISSE: Do be reasonable; I know where the *towels* are.

VENTROUX: To hell with the towels!—What is it you are trying to prove? That a mother has every right to parade before her son stark naked?

CLARISSE: That's not what I'm saying.—My, my you get so heated.

VENTROUX: You'd be heated if someone threw your brains into a pot of boiling water.

CLARISSE: Just calm down and try to explain yourself without getting in a state. I promise to listen very attentively.

VENTROUX: The thing is, Clarisse, and this has become more and more clear to me as time has gone on, you can't *help* traipsing around without clothes on. It's a disease. Something beyond your control.

CLARISSE: Now you're just being stupid again.

VENTROUX: I have to mention it every day. Every single day. Without fail!

CLARISSE: That's nonsense. Occasionally in the mornings, when I'm not yet dressed, perhaps, but once I am dressed I can assure you —

VENTROUX: —that you're no longer in your nightie? Yes, true! But you never *get* dressed. It never happens.

CLARISSE: Would you prefer I didn't wash or have a shower?

VENTROUX: Wash yourself, by all means. Shower to your heart's content. But stay inside your room. Close the door. *You never close the door!* The servants are always getting a free strip-show.

CLARISSE: They never come in.

VENTROUX: They don't have to. The view is perfect from the outside.

CLARISSE: Do you really believe the servants watch me!?

VENTROUX: Watch you? They *ogle* you! They *drool* over you! They may sell tickets for all I know. Odd, you always leave the door open when you shower but you shut yourself in—as if in a cloister—when you put on your veil.

CLARISSE: *(Suddenly twitching as if some sensitive nerve has been tweaked.)* I can't bear being disturbed when I put on my veil. If there are people around, it drives me mad. Quite, quite mad!

VENTROUX: It's unfortunate you don't feel the same way about your ablutions. But as if that weren't bad enough, you always turn on all the lights in the bathroom and you never—*never ever*—draw the blinds.

CLARISSE: Oh, this is ridiculous!

VENTROUX: Yesterday! What about yesterday?

CLARISSE: *(Guiltily admitting it.)* Oh well, yesterday…yesterday was —

VENTROUX: — like every other day! A public exhibition! You're like an ostrich. Because you can't see outside, you think no one can see inside.

CLARISSE: Who is there to look anyway?

VENTROUX: *Clemenceau*, that's who! Clemenceau who lives directly across the way and who is always at his window. And why not? The curtain never falls, so why should the public depart?

CLARISSE: Who cares anyway! I've nothing Clemenceau hasn't seen before.

VENTROUX: Clemenceau is a curmudgeon! A devil! All he needs is the slightest bit of rope and he'll hang me with it. He'll concoct some vicious little gossip about me and spread it all over town and I'll be ruined.

CLARISSE: But Clemenceau is a member of your own party.

VENTROUX: That's the whole point! One's most vicious enemies are always in one's own party. If Clemenceau belonged to the Left, I wouldn't give a damn.

Nor would he. But since we are both on the same side, we are bitter rivals. Clemenceau knows very well he could be made a Delegate. As could I.

CLARISSE: *(Surprized.)* You?

VENTROUX: Yes, I! Is that so incredible? You know very well that during the last Cabinet shake-up, after I gave that brilliant speech about the spread of porkbellies, I was approached by the Steering Committee and offered the Ministry of the Navy.

CLARISSE: You were?

VENTROUX: I was! Minister of the Navy.—Not bad, ey?

CLARISSE: But you don't even know how to swim!

VENTROUX: So what? The Minister of Transport doesn't know how to drive! The Minister of Finance doesn't know how to count! And the Minister of Health is suffering from a sexually-transmitted disease which will no doubt polish him off before the next Session.

CLARISSE: Ah then, I suppose you're in with a chance.

VENTROUX: I don't know why I even bother to discuss these things with you. A man's greatness is never recognized at home. Thank God those that hardly know me have a different opinion. *(Turning to her earnestly.)* So you see, you mustn't sabotage my chances by putting me into a compromising situation—with Clemenceau—or anyone else. It might bring dire consequences. You must never forget that you are married to a man with an unlimited political future. How would it sit with the government if they discovered that a Minister of State has a wife who traipses through the house without clothes on?

CLARISSE: Not good?

VENTROUX: Disastrous, Clarisse, disastrous! And you know, the wonderful thing about this regime is anyone can aspire to become President of the Republic. And if such an honor befell me, well just consider for a moment…We'd have to entertain Kings, Queens, Foreign Dignitaries. Would you officiate at such occasions wearing a transparent nightie?

CLARISSE: Certainly not.

VENTROUX: Is this how you would meet foreign Heads-of-State?

CLARISSE: Of course not. —I would put on my lace dressing-gown with the gold cupids.

VENTROUX: *(Taking his head in both hands and rocking in pain.)* Her dressing-gown-with-the-gold-cupids!

CLARISSE: *(Losing patience.)* Oh, I'll put on whatever you want!

VENTROUX: My sweet little child. It really is alarming. You have absolutely no sense of decorum, have you?

CLARISSE: *(Indignant.)* Me? No sense of decorum?

VENTROUX: *(Taking hold of her shoulders, tenderly.)* I don't resent you for it. You're just an innocent little babe. You simply don't understand the ways of the world

CLARISSE: All right, give me one example. One example of my lack of decorum, as you call it.

VENTROUX: We won't have to look further than yesterday. When M'sieur Deschanel came to call.

CLARISSE: Deschanel?—What?

VENTROUX: You hadn't been introduced to him five minutes and you took hold of his trousers and said: "What a curious piece of fabric that is. What could it be?"—And then you began rubbing his thighs. *(He demonstrates the action.)*

CLARISSE: His thighs. I cared nothing for his thighs; I was only feeling the fabric.

VENTROUX: Yes, but his thighs were underneath the fabric. —Do you think that was a discreet thing to do?

CLARISSE: What else *should* I have done? I couldn't very well ask him to take his pants off and pass them over. Not with a man I'd just met.

VENTROUX: Couldn't you just restrain your curiosity, Clarisse, and refrained from stroking the material.

CLARISSE: *He* didn't seem to mind. He seemed to be enjoying it.

VENTROUX: That's not the point, Clarisse! You don't go up to a man you've just met and begin stroking his thighs! Deschanel is an illustrious political figure with a significant record of achievement. Surely you could have found another topic of conversation—other than his trousers.

CLARISSE: Oh, you see the worst side of everything. And you are in no position to criticize me.—My "lack of decorum!" What about yours? At the picnic last week, with Mademoiselle Dieumamour? You thought I was in the house, but I saw you quite clearly.

VENTROUX: What are you going on about, Mademoiselle Dieumamour?

CLARISSE: You were sucking her neck. In full sight of everyone. Was that respectable behavior?

VENTROUX: Oh God defend us if the history books ever get written by the women.

CLARISSE: Can you deny you were sucking her neck?

VENTROUX: *(Emphatically.)* Yes, I sucked her neck! *Undeniably* I sucked her neck, and I'll shout it from the rooftops and tell the world I did so.—And I am proud of it!

CLARISSE: Really?

VENTROUX: Surely you don't imagine I was attracted by her superannuated, crumbling body and those little black pot-holes decorating her nose…
CLARISSE: Men are so perverse, it's impossible to say what gives them a thrill!
VENTROUX: The fact is the poor woman was stung by a giant wasp and the bite looked as if it might be infected. It was already red and swollen. Surely, I couldn't stand by and allow the poor lady to suffer—just for the sake of propriety.
CLARISSE: How could you tell the bite was infected?
VENTROUX: A wasp bite can be fatal if it isn't cauterized at once or someone doesn't suck out the poison from the wound. There was no way of cauterizing it, so I did the only thing I could do. I was motivated by the principle of Christian charity and so…I sucked!
CLARISSE: How convenient for you. By that kind of reasoning, you can justify sucking on any woman's neck that you believe has been stung by a bee or a horsefly.
VENTROUX: You can't believe I did it for pleasure?!
CLARISSE: Oh no, no.
VENTROUX: I practically choked on the smell of stale powder and old soap. I think I deserve some commendation for bravery beyond the call of duty.
CLARISSE: Oh yes, when others do things like that, it's always wrong, but when you do it, then it's "bravery beyond the call of duty."
VENTROUX: I'm not saying any such thing.
CLARISSE: If you'd found *me* sucking on some old gentleman's neck, I'd never hear the end of it.
VENTROUX: Naturally, I'd be upset.
CLARISSE: You see, *you'd* be upset, but I'm supposed to be understanding.
VENTROUX: *(Sizes her up for a moment, contemplates her childishness, and then draws her close to him.)* You have a disarming way of starting an argument, my dear.
CLARISSE: What are you talking about?
VENTROUX: You're right. You're always right. And I swear to you: that is the first and last time I will ever suck Mademoiselle Dieumamour's neck.
CLARISSE: I don't mean that. If she were to be stung again, the poor woman, your duty as a man would be to…
VENTROUX: Ah, then you *do* agree with me!
CLARISSE: *(Close to him and beginning to soften.)* How maddening you are. Always saying things to hurt my feelings. And when I try to defend myself, I wind up being utterly confused.
VENTROUX: I, hurtful things?

CLARISSE: That I walk around naked and suck old gentleman's necks.
VENTROUX: I never said any such thing.
CLARISSE: You said I was stroking that man's thighs.
VENTROUX: When you do things I disapprove of, I think I have the right to mention them, wouldn't you say?
CLARISSE: *(On his lap.)* I'm not saying you don't, but you don't have to be so strict about it. You know when you talk nicely to me, you can get me to do whatever you want.
VENTROUX: Very well then. And in the nicest manner possible: *(Sweetly.)* Please stop walking around without clothes on.
CLARISSE: You see, you can be kind and gentle.
VENTROUX: Then we're all made up. *(They kiss.)*
CLARISSE: *(Head on his shoulder.)* You see how reasonable I can be when you're nice to me.
(VICTOR suddenly barges into the room and encounters CLARISSE in her see-through nightie seated on VENTROUX's lap.)
VICTOR: Oh!
CLARISSE: *(Turning suddenly.)* Oh!
(She leaps up and towards the window bumping VICTOR who has turned his back.)
VENTROUX: Who's that?
VICTOR *(Still turned away.)* Only me, sir.
CLARISSE: *(By the window, covers herself with the curtain.)* Don't look—don't look!
VICTOR: *(Blasé, who has already had an eyeful.)* No ma'am.
VENTROUX: *(Beginning to boil again.)* It's a little late for "Don't look—Don't look."
CLARISSE: *(Trying to pacify him.)* Well I am behind the curtain!
VENTROUX: He's already seen the whole kaboodle.
CLARISSE: Keep a civil tongue in your head!
VICTOR: *(Still blasé.)* Oh really, sir, it's not as if I'm a new man in the house…
VENTROUX: So it's not the first time he's seen you in the altogether!—Delightful!
CLARISSE: Darling, I assure you…
VENTROUX: Oh, just drop it. It's too painful to discuss.
VICTOR: *(Trying to be agreeable.)* Not to worry, really. Back at the house…
VENTROUX: "Back at the house…" I can just imagine what's been going on "back at the house." —What audacity!
VICTOR: But, sir, all I…
VENTROUX: What are you doing here anyway? Didn't I tell you to get out?

VICTOR: I just came to tell you about the visitor, sir. He dropped off his card.
VENTROUX: *(Snatches the card out of VICTOR's hand.)* Who? *(Reads it again.)* No, it's impossible. I can't believe it. Him here?—Never!
VICTOR: It's "him" all right.
VENTROUX: *(Calling him back to order.)* What "him"? Who "him."
VICTOR: *(Chastened.)* Him! The same. He said he'd be back at four-thirty.
VENTROUX: *(Smiling slyly, hatching something.)* Back at four thirty, ey. Well, we'll see about that. *(Catching VICTOR nodding and smiling as himself.)* What are *you* smiling at?
VICTOR: *(The smile wiped from his face.)* I've no idea, sir.
VENTROUX: *(Barking.)* Get the hell out of here!
(VICTOR bolts out. CLARISSE comes out from behind the curtain and heaves a sigh of relief.)
VENTROUX: *(Reflecting on his visitor.)* I'm not at all put out by this unexpected development.
CLARISSE: Oh, I'm so glad to hear that. I thought you might be upset.
VENTROUX: *(Infuriated her misinterpretation.)* Of course I'm upset. Violently upset!
CLARISSE: I thought you just said you *weren't*.
VENTROUX: I'm not upset at what's happened to you. I quite relish that. Maybe it will finally teach you a lesson.
CLARISSE: But I thought we'd agreed to be nice to each other.
VENTROUX: I let down my guard for a moment and this is what happens!
CLARISSE: It's not the end of the world, darling.—Who left the card?
VENTROUX: You'd never know if it *were* the end of the world. You'd be too busy washing or showering to notice.
CLARISSE: Don't be a brute.—Whose card is that??
VENTROUX: What business is it of yours?
CLARISSE: *(Mock offended.)* Well, excuse me! I only live here, you know.
VENTROUX: I know that—Everyone in the neighborhood knows it now!
CLARISSE: *(Fiercely curious.)* Whose calling card is that!!?
VENTROUX: If you really want to know, ma chere Clarisse, it is a man before whom we are very fortunate you did not exhibit yourself in that flimsy piece of camouflage with which you flaunted yourself before Victor. Had he been witness to that scene, as far as my future is concerned, my goose would have been cooked.
CLARISSE: Why is that?
VENTROUX: Because if I gave him the tiniest little title to use against me, it would be the end of my political career. *La Commedia è finita!*

CLARISSE: *(Craning to read the card.)* Is he an Italian?
VENTROUX: *(Barking.)* No, he's not an Italian. He's the man who ruthlessly campaigned against me at the last election and did his level best to throw me to the wolves.
CLARISSE: *(It dawning upon her.)* Not Petard Himmelfaahrt?
VENTROUX: The very man. The venomous Mayor of Moussilon-les-Indrets!
CLARISSE: That scoundrel did everything in his power to boost your opponent, the Marquise of Berneville.
VENTROUX: The slimy Socialist *cochon*, may he rot in hell.
CLARISSE: He called you a prig, a snob—
VENTROUX: *(Smoldering with recollected anger.)* … and "a finagling parasite."
CLARISSE: *(After a thought.)* But is that so wrong?
VENTROUX: *(Fuming.)* So wrong!?
CLARISSE: I mean you *are* a Parisite. You were born in Montparnasse.
VENTROUX: *(Controlling his rising blood temperature.)* And so…I…am…a…Paris-Ite.
CLARISSE: And you've always lived in Paris.
VENTROUX: *(Between gritted teeth.)* And so…I…am…a…Paris-Ite.
CLARISSE: I don't see why you should take umbrage at that. He might have said far worse things. That you're a terrible grouch for instance; that you're always flying off the handle and that, in the mornings, your halitosis is terrible. *(A new thought.)* Then again, why should he attack you at all? It's extremely rude of him. Intolerable, in fact. —Who asked him for his opinion anyway?— I'd like to give him a piece of my mind.
VENTROUX: Let us be frugal, Clarisse. It's not as if there's all that much to go around.
CLARISSE: The more I think of it, the angrier I get. You should show him to the door as soon as he arrives, and then slam it shut behind him!
VENTROUX: *(His plan hatched.)* Au contraire, Clarisse. I will be as pleasant as I possibly can. And *(Emphatically.)* *so will you!*
CLARISSE: I will?
VENTROUX: It is a perfect opportunity for revenge, Clarisse. Even though he is a low-brow, beady-eyed rodent of the first water, you must remember he is a well-respected entrepreneur. His textile mill employs over six hundred workers, which means *six hundred votes*, Clarisse. You must be sickeningly pleasant to him at all costs, and we must humor him. *(Looking at his watch.)* He'll be here any moment. Go, go get dressed! *(CLARISSE goes to pull the bell-cord.)* What are you doing?
CLARISSE: Ringing for Victor.

VENTROUX: *(Acridly.)* Hasn't he seen enough this afternoon?
CLARISSE: *(Beating the air as if spanking her husband.)* Naughty boy!—It's so's he can clear away the tray. I've told him twenty times to clear away the cups and saucers when we are done with our morning coffee. It's disgusting to have things like that lying about. It attracts bees and mosquitoes. *(She shoos them away from the coffee things.)* I cannot bear *mess*. I must have order in my home.
VENTROUX: *(Of his wife's nightie.) She* must have order!
CLARISSE: And since I don't want Victor to see me like this...
VENTROUX: *(Mockingly.)* Oh, you don't?
CLARISSE: Don't tease; you know very well I don't. When he comes, make sure he clears all these things away, will you?
VENTROUX: There's no point in tugging at the bell, Clarisse. It hasn't worked for days. There is something wrong with the battery.
CLARISSE: It's probably parched—with all this heat. Just give it a little water.
VENTROUX: *(Patronizingly.)* Yes, a little liquid refreshment. Just what it needs. *(A bark.)* For God's sake, put some clothes on!!!
CLARISSE: *(Sugary sweet.)* How can anyone resist you cherie, when you ask so sweetly. *(Exits.)*

(After closing the door, something catches VENTROUX's eye at the window that, being without its blind, is still wide open. VENTROUX focuses on something only he can see. He sidles past the window casually then furtively doubles back on himself and then leaps directly in front of the glass, performing a monstrous pantomime.)

VENTROUX: I see you, Clemenceau, you old pervert! I see you peering into our window! Have you nothing better to do with your time? No, I don't suppose so. *(Crying out.)* Voyeur! Pervert!! ANARCHIST! *(Impulsively, he turns his rear end towards the window, flaunting his disdain. At that moment, the doorbell rings.)* Ah, now comes the other scoundrel!
(Having said this, he restores his aplomb and with great dignity awaits the arrival of his guest.)
VICTOR: M'sieur Himmelfaahrt. *(Pronounced "himmelfar"—without the "t.")*

(PETARD HIMMELFAAHRT, a stuffy, burly man in his fifties, enters guardedly.)

VENTROUX: Do come in, I was expecting you.
HIMMELFAAHRT: Ah Ventroux, good day.

VENTROUX: *(Imperiously, to VICTOR.)* You may leave us now.
(VICTOR, unaccustomed to VENTROUX's aristocratic manner, shoots him a quizzical look and is waived out of the room.)
VENTROUX: Do sit down, Monsieur Himmelfaahrt. *(He pronounces the last syllable with a deliberately hard "t" sound.)*
HIMMELFAAHRT: *(Correcting him.)* Himmel*faahr*.
(During the course of the scene, VENTROUX will several times make to sit, which impels HIMMELFAAHRT to do the same, but at the very last instant, VENTROUX will not sit nor will HIMMELFAAHRT. This sitting-standing game will go on throughout the scene.)
HIMMELFAAHRT: My dear friend…
VENTROUX: *(Coldly imperious.)* "Dear"? A strange adjective from your lips given the tenor of the campaign you recently waged against me, M'sieur Himmelfaahrt.
HIMMELFAAHRT: *(Gently correcting him.)* Himmel*faahr*.—Ah well, in the heat of the campaign…
VENTROUX: Many are painfully scalded, are they not, M'sieurHimmelfaahrt? *(About to sit, doesn't.)*
HIMMELFAAHRT: *(Also about to sit, doesn't.)* Himmel*faahr*.—Well, well, you know what they say about the heat in the kitchen.
VENTROUX: I was not *in the kitchen*, I was at the political rallies. What have kitchens to do with it, M'sieur Himmelfaahrt?
HIMMELFAAHRT: *(Gently correcting him.)* Himmel*faahr*.
VENTROUX: You accused me of being a traitor, an embezzler, a snob, a pig and an incorrigible decadent!
HIMMELFAAHRT: *(Amiably.)* Which in no way reflected the esteem in which I hold you.
VENTROUX: *(Rattled.)* Ey?
HIMMELFAAHRT: I must admit I was not one of your staunchest supporters. But then, I was obliged to back the Marquis de Berneville.
VENTROUX: Of course, you are perfectly at liberty to back whomever you like—no matter how fatuous your choice may be. *(About to sit, doesn't.)*
HIMMELFAAHRT: *(Ditto.)* He's a very old friend, you know. He was at my daughter's baptism, stood godfather to my son, was with me at the military academy and happens to be the sixth richest man in France, which is a glowing commendation for any politician.
VENTROUX: You needn't justify yourself to me, M'sieur Himmelfaahrt.
HIMMELFAAHRT: *(Gently correcting.)* Himmel*faahr*. Nevertheless, M'sieur, it was you who won the election.

VENTROUX: Which ultimately, is the only thing that counts.
(He is about to sit, but doesn't. HIMMELFAAHRT does the same. Then, suddenly, VENTROUX moves to a seat and HIMMELFAAHRT, sensing the move, sits at exactly the same instant.)
HIMMELFAAHRT: In any case, that is all water under the bridge, or as you might say, mud down the sewer hole. I come to you as the Mayor of Moussillon-les-Indrets paying a friendly visit to his representative in Parliament and to convey the warmest greetings of his entire constituency. I felt sure that, no matter what had gone before, I would be well-received.
VENTROUX: And so you are, M'sieur Himmelfaahrt. In fact, I was just saying to my wife a few moments earlier…
HIMMELFAAHRT: I am sorry not to have asked after her earlier. I do hope I will have the pleasure of meeting Madame at some point.
VENTROUX: *(Speaking so that CLARISSE can hear.)* Unfortunately, my wife is dressing at the moment, and you know with women, that can sometimes take an inordinately long time.
HIMMELFAAHRT: I will be sorry to have missed her.
CLARISSE: *(Offstage. Screeching.)* So that's what you call clearing the dishes, is it? *(Sound of dishes clattering to the floor.)*
VENTROUX: *(Trying to talk over his wife's voice.)* Then again, I may be mistaken. One can never predict a woman's arrival, can one? I think I can just barely make out her voice.—Already dressed! Quite astounding.
HIMMELFAAHRT: Then I may have the pleasure after all…
(CLARISSE comes flying out of her room, still wearing the transparent nightie, and followed by a terrified VICTOR. VENTROUX, seeing the sight, jumps out of his skin.)
CLARISSE: Look at those coffee cups, rotting away on the table.
VENTROUX: Oghh!
(VENTROUX's cry startles CLARISSE who immediately does an about-face, bumping into VICTOR who drops his tray as CLARISSE stumbles over him.)
VENTROUX: *(Rushing over to her, sotto voce.)* Will you please get the hell out of here!
CLARISSE: What's the matter?
VENTROUX: Are you mad, coming out here like that in the middle of company?!
CLARISSE: *(Over VENTROUX's shoulder, to HIMMELFAAHRT.)* Oh, I beg your pardon, sir. I didn't hear you ring.
HIMMELFAAHRT: *(Cavalier.)* Think nothing of it, Madame.
VENTROUX: *(In hushed tones, trying to conceal his wife.)* Have you no shame? Showing yourself like that in public? Barking at the servant!

CLARISSE: *(In hushed tones, unaware of the impropriety.)* It's just that Victor hadn't cleared away the mess. *(To Victor.)* I told you three times to clear away the coffee cups!

VENTROUX: *(Going mad.)* Damn the coffee cups! *(To VICTOR.)* You, get the hell out of here! *(Pushes VICTOR backwards out of the room.)*

CLARISSE: *(Moving towards HIMMELFAAHRT who instinctively draws away while VENTROUX whispers to VICTOR up-stage.)* I don't know if you feel the same, but when I see a pile of dirty dishes, it just drives me to distraction. I can't explain it. It just does.

VENTROUX: *(Shooing his wife up-stage in a harsh whisper.)* Get out, get out! Shoo! Shoo!

CLARISSE: *(Breaking free from his grasp.)* Stop talking to me as if I were a dog!

(VENTROUX, who is in agony, twists and turns between his wife, his visitor and VICTOR, finally shoving his servant out the door.)

CLARISSE: *(Pleasantly approaching HIMMELFAAHRT, the perfect hostess.)* You are M'sieur Himmelfaahrt, are you not?

HIMMELFAAHRT: *(Correcting.)* Himmel*faahr*...

CLARISSE: Do take a seat. I've heard so much about you from my husband, and others of course. *(HIMMELFAAHRT, his eyes glued to her breasts, is startled when she asks.)* Would you like a little bite? *(As he looks up, she offers the fruit bowl. HIMMELFAAHRT involuntarily recoils.)*

VENTROUX: *(Through gritted teeth.)* Surely you are not going to play the hostess dressed like that, darling?

CLARISSE: *(Not really perturbed.)* No, I suppose it is slightly improper.

VENTROUX: *(To himself, boiling over.)* Slightly improper.

CLARISSE: But it is roasting hot. *(Places both her hands on HIMMELFAAHRT's, which are flat on the table.)* Just feel these hands. I think I've got a fever.

VENTROUX: There you go again. Just like with Deschanel!

CLARISSE: What are you talking about? I'm touching his hands not his thighs!

(HIMMELFAAHRT darts his hands away and looks confused.)

VENTROUX: The man couldn't care less about your hands!

HIMMELFAAHRT: On the contrary, M'sieur; they are very lovely hands.

CLARISSE: You see.

VENTROUX: Enough, enough. Leave us at once!

CLARISSE: Very well. But I'm only trying to humor him like you asked me to.

VENTROUX: I,—asked you to humor him?—What are you saying??!
CLARISSE: Didn't you just tell me a few moments ago, I was to be "sickeningly pleasant" to M'sieur Himmelfaahrt?
VENTROUX: *(Caught in his own trap, whisperingly.)* All right, all right, all right!
CLARISSE: It's not "all right." One moment you say "humor the man" "be sickeningly pleasant" and when I try to do just that, you rail and scream and…
VENTROUX: *(Trying to exonerate himself before HIMMELFAAHRT.)* I never said any such thing. You misunderstood.
CLARISSE: Didn't you say he was a low-brow beady-eyed rodent of the first water… *(HIMMELFAAHRT turns sharply to VENTROUX.)* …that he employed over six hundred employees…that we had to humor him…that—
VENTROUX: I never said anything of the sort. You're delusional! You need treatment. Sedation! *(To HIMMELFAAHRT.)* I hope you don't believe that I could possibly have uttered words like that about a respected colleague and civic leader who…
HIMMELFAAHRT: Ah well, we all use odd expressions sometimes…
VENTROUX: Never, in a million years, could I have spoken such things!
CLARISSE: *(To HIMMELFAAHRT.)* I hope you don't think I'm the sort of person that would make up lies about…
VENTROUX: *(Erupting.)* I've had just about enough of you. *(Points to the door.)* Out! Just get the hell out of here!
CLARISSE: How dare you use that tone of voice to me?!
VENTROUX: *(Refusing to listen.)* Out, out, out!! Vacate the premises at once!
CLARISSE: Don't you remember we had this conversation not five minutes ago when you said…
VENTROUX: Hop it, hop it!
CLARISSE: If you can't remember what you've said from one moment to the next, how can one possibly…
VENTROUX: *(Threateningly.)* Are you going to make an exit or not!?

(He drags her to the door, pushes her out and slams it shut. He then turns on a genial smile for HIMMELFAAHRT's benefit but almost immediately, CLARISSE returns.)

CLARISSE: I never did get a chance to say good-bye, M'sieur Himmelfaahrt. I'm very pleased to have made your…
(In a flash, VENTROUX has twirled her out of the room as if she had never reappeared. He then approaches HIMMLEFAAHRT.)
VENTROUX: I cannot possibly express how mortified I am, M'sieur

Himmelfaahr. (He makes a point of pronouncing it correctly). The fact is my wife is a fanciful creature who suffers from delusions from time to time. It runs in her family, I fear. Her mother was a certified lunatic—or so her father told me—although he himself was under the impression that he was the reincarnation of Napoleon Bonaparte. In his last years, he was totally cured but refused to remove the three-cornered hat he wore on every occasion and insisted on being buried at Saint Helena which, since he was still alive and in perfectly good health, was naturally out of the question.

HIMMELFAAHRT: Ah well, we all have our crosses to bear.

VENTROUX: It is just incredible the things that pop into her head out of her mouth. "Low-brow beady-eyed rodent…" is really one of her more extraordinary concoctions. At other times, of course, she behaves quite normally.

HIMMELFAAHRT: We all use language we may sometimes regret, M'sieur Ventoux. Didn't I myself call you a prig or a snob or somesuch during the recent elections?

VENTROUX: "Finagling parasite," I believe was the term in question.

HIMMELFAAHRT: Ah, yes,—quite good that.

VENTROUX: And you must forgive my wife the manner in which she presented herself.

HIMMELFAAHRT: Very picturesque I thought.

VENTROUX: You are extremely courteous to excuse her…her…excesses. I can assure you she's not in the habit of walking around like that. It is, of course, quite warm today which almost—but not quite—excuses her inexcusable behavior. You felt her hands I'm sure.

HIMMELFAAHRT: Yes, yes.

VENTROUX: It is very humid today. Here, just feel mine *(Takes one of HIMMELFAAHRT's hands between his own.)* Quite damp as you see.

HIMMELFAAHRT: *(Withdrawing his hand and wiping it on his shirt.)* Yes, yes, I see.

VENTROUX: And quite unpleasant.

HIMMELFAAHRT: *(Still drying his hand.)* Very unpleasant indeed.

VENTROUX: And so naturally, being flushed and humid and *drenched* in fact, my wife felt the need to change into her…her "thing."

HIMMELFAAHRT: Quite understandable.

VENTROUX: It is, isn't it? Removing one's clothes on such a day.

HIMMELFAAHRT: *(Lightheartedly.)* If only I could do the same.

VENTROUX: *(Without thinking.)* By all means, do.

HIMMELFAAHRT: *(Shocked at the suggestion, sharply.)* What did you say?

VENTROUX: *(Trying to extricate himself.)* No, I mean *don't*. I mean we *can't!*

Obviously, it's out of the question! — And then of course, not having heard the bell or knowing you were here, she just walked in with her… *(Mimes "her breasts.")*

HIMMELFAAHRT: Naturally…and the servant who was with her…?

VENTROUX: *(Disconcerted.)* The servant?—Ah yes, that must have looked very peculiar, but the fact is there's a very simple explanation for that.

HIMMELFAAHRT: Ah, yes?

VENTROUX: If it was just a "normal servant," then obviously it would be…

HIMMELFAAHRT: Obviously, obviously…

VENTROUX: But the fact is, she and this servant, they were brought up together.

HIMMELFAAHRT: Really?

VENTROUX: Practically brother and sister. They played together; studied together; bathed together —no, no, I'm not quite sure about *that*—but the fact is, they were inseparable throughout their childhood.

HIMMELFAAHRT: Ah well, that explains a good deal.

VENTROUX: A quite remarkable intimacy…*(Thinking better of that.)* or as one might say "close-knit friendship." *(Wanting to change the subject.)* But in any case, what exactly is the purpose of your visit? What exactly is it you wanted to discuss?

HIMMELFAAHRT: Well let's get right down to it. It's about the Paris Express; the one that stops at Morinville, as you know, but does *not* stop at Mousillon-les-Indrets which, if you think about it, is an equally important center of commerce and industry.

VENTROUX: Certainly, certainly.

HIMMELFAAHRT: That being the case, the residents in our area are of the mind that the Express *should* stop at Mousillon-les-Indrets.

VENTROUX: *(Nodding in the affirmative.)* Certainly, certainly. *(Then shaking his head negatively.)* Then again, that would be rather difficult, quite impossible in fact.

HIMMELFAAHRT: But we've had two instances of it happening.

VENTROUX: The Express has stopped there?

HIMMELFAAHRT: Twice! Once following a derailment, and the second time after someone had sabotaged the track.

VENTROUX: I see.

HIMMELFAAHRT: The problem is, those were what you might call "irregular stops." The passengers cannot depend on them—unless of course they engineer the derailments and sabotage themselves, which would be very time consuming, as you can imagine.

VENTROUX: I quite see that. —So you would prefer to have a scheduled stop.

HIMMELFAAHRT: Exactly. To avoid the bother of derailments or sabotage.

VENTROUX: Certainly, certainly. —I'll tell you what I'll do. I need to draft a short proposal about this. But in the meantime, so that it doesn't slip my mind, I'll just write myself a memo, as I usually do. *(Takes out pad and starts writing.)* "Scheduled stops"…"Paris Express"…"Mousillon-les-Indrets"… M'sieur Petard Himm-el-*fart*.

HIMMELFAAHRT: *(Who has been looking over his shoulder.)* No, no, that's not it. Himmel-FAAHR…*(Lyrically.)* F—A—A—H—R silent—T.

VENTROUX: *(Spelling it out.)* Not F—A—R —T…

HIMMELFAAHRT: No, no.

VENTROUX: I'm so sorry.

HIMMELFAAHRT: Not to worry; that *is* the first thing that comes to mind.

VENTROUX: Naturally.

HIMMELFAAHRT: Of course.

VENTROUX: *(Reminding himself.)* Silent—T.

HIMMELFAAHRT: *(Demonstrating musically.)* Faaaaaaahrrrr…

VENTROUX & HIMMELFAAHRT: *(Together.)* Faaaaahrrrrr…

(The sound of the strained voices of CLARISSE and VICTOR are suddenly heard behind the door.)

VICTOR: *(Offstage.)* Is your leg up?

CLARISSE: *(Offstage.)* I've got both legs up. Have you got your hand around it?

VICTOR: *(Offstage. Grunting.)* I've got both hands around it.

(HIMMELFAAHRT and VENTROUX look to one another with dread.)

CLARISSE: *(Offstage.)* Can't you get it any tighter?

VICTOR: *(Offstage.) (Breathing heavily.)* It's about as tight as I can get it.

CLARISSE: *(Offstage.)* It's pretty hot but I'll pass it over.

VICTOR: *(Offstage.)* Do hurry Madame, I don't know if I can keep it up.

(Another shared look of dismay between HIMMELFAAHRT and VENTROUX.)

CLARISSE: *(Offstage.)* It's coming…it's coming.

(VENTROUX, unable to contain himself any longer, jerks open the door to discover his wife perched precariously on top of the stepladder. Only half her body is in view with VICTOR on the bottom step, holding CLARISSE from behind around the waist. VENTROUX emits a short shriek and instinctively takes a step back.)

CLARISSE: *(Hearing her husband's shriek, she bends down and her head comes into view. She is holding a hot-water bottle and VICTOR is holding her around her hips.) (Casually, to VENTROUX.)* Oh, it's you.

VENTROUX: *(Aghast.)* What are you doing up there!?

CLARISSE: *(Nonchalantly.)* Just fixing the battery.

VENTROUX: *(Fuming, to VICTOR.)* And you!! Is that any way to hold Madame Ventroux?

VICTOR: It's just so that she won't fall.

VENTROUX: What?

CLARISSE: If someone doesn't hold me, I get dizzy.

VENTROUX: Can't you see that you have both hands on her…her… It's positively indecent! For God's sake, *take your hands away!! (He pushes VICTOR aside.)*

CLARISSE: *(Wobbling.)* I'm going to fall; I'm going to fall.

VENTROUX: *(Pulling her down.)* Get down. What *are* you thinking of? That's no job for you!

CLARISSE: *(Climbing down and passing the hot-water bottle to VICTOR.)* He has no idea how to do it.

VENTROUX: Let him learn then! — And still in that…that…"thing." *(Cruelly ironic.)* Very tasteful, I'm sure. And in front of the servant!

HIMMELFAAHRT: Well, they are virtually brother and sister.

(VENTROUX winces as his own words return to him.)

CLARISSE: *(Turning to VICTOR.)* Who?

VICTOR: *(Turning to CLARISSE.)* Me?

VENTROUX: Yes you! *(Pushes VICTOR back which sends him into the stepladder and almost onto the floor.)* Just get out of here, will you. Who asked you to meddle in all this?

VICTOR: Madame asked me to…

VENTROUX: Out, out! *(He slams the door on him.)* I'm going to give that man two weeks notice and dismiss him first thing in the morning. *(Turning to HIMMELFAAHRT who stands looking quizzically.)* They *are* like brother and sister but more like half-brother and half-sister.

HIMMELFAAHRT: Half-brother and half-sister???

VENTROUX: I mean—more like distant cousins…or nephew and niece…or… *(Exasperated at his inability to find an appropriate explanation, he finally explodes.)* You know, your damned questions are beginning to get my goat! What business is it of yours anyway?

HIMMELFAAHRT: But…but…

VENTROUX: Surely if I tolerate such behavior, I must have good reasons for it.

HIMMELFAAHRT: But I've said nothing about it!

VENTROUX: Yes, but I know damn well what's going on in your head. No, you say nothing but once you're out there with the Marquis, you'll start blabbering to every journalist in town.

HIMMELFAAHRT: But where do you get such an idea?

CLARISSE: *(To VENTROUX, with concern.)* I tell you, my dear, you should really consider getting some medical help.

VENTROUX: *(Furious.)* ARE YOU EVER GOING TO GET DRESSED?!

CLARISSE: Give me a moment, will you?

VENTROUX: A moment! A moment! It's been a full hour since you first flaunted yourself in that…that "thing!"

CLARISSE: Well what's so terrible? M'sieur Himmelfaahrt has already seen everything there is to see.—*(Turning to HIMMELFAAHRT.)* I ask you M'sieur: is this "thing" any more revealing than you would see on any stage in Paris?

HIMMELFAAHRT: Not at all, Madame. At the Folies Bergere, this would be quite a modest display.

VENTROUX: THIS IS NOT THE FOLIES BERGERE, THIS IS MY HOME!

CLARISSE: Mine too.

VENTROUX: *(Panics, seeing her before the window).* You're standing right in front of the window—in full view of Clemenceau! *(He pushes her away from the window and makes obscene gestures out the window.)*

HIMMELFAAHRT: *(Concerned about his sanity, turns to CLARISSE and whispers.)* Does he often have these attacks?

(CLARISSE lets out a piercing scream and jumps a full foot into the air. Both VENTROUX and HIMMELFAAHRT jump out of their skins.)

VENTROUX: What now?

CLARISSE: A dagger. I felt a dagger go right through my heart.
(As she speaks, she turns and we see a crushed wasp on her nightie just by her backside.)

VENTROUX: You have a rather odd sense of direction, Clarisse. Here's your dagger. It's just a wasp sting. *(Smashes it underfoot.)*

CLARISSE: *(Hysterically.)* A wasp! A wasp. I've been stung by a wasp!

HIMMELFAAHRT: How dreadful!

VENTROUX: *(Throwaway.)* That'll teach you to walk around bare-assed.

CLARISSE: *(Pointing to the coffee cup.)* There, I told you what would happen if you left the dirty dishes lying around. I told you so! *(Suddenly panicked at the thought.)* What if it's…poisonous? — What if the poison is this very minute entering my bloodstream!?

VENTROUX: Don' be stupid.
CLARISSE: *(Rushing to VENTROUX.)* Oh Julien, please, suck it! Suck it!
VENTROUX: Me? Don't look at me!
CLARISSE: Oh Julien, I beg of you. Suck me, suck me!
VENTROUX: You're behaving like a madwoman.
CLARISSE: Suck it, suck it. You sucked Mademoiselle Dieumamour.
   (HIMMELFAAHRT who has been trying to maintain a discreet silence, suddenly whips around and confronts VENTROUX accusingly.)
VENTROUX: Stop being stupid, Clarisse.
CLARISSE: *(Still panicked.)* Oh, you are so cruel, Julien. *(Turns suddenly to HIMMELFAAHRT who, sensing what is coming, grows pale.)*—M'sieur Himmelfaahrt.
HIMMELFAAHRT: *(Quaking.)* Mad-ame…
CLARISSE: Please M'sieur Himmelfaahrt, please!
VENTROUX: Have you totally lost your senses. Asking M'sieur Himmelfaahrt to…
CLARISSE: I'd rather do that than risk death.
HIMMELFAAHRT: *(Ever the gentleman.)* I am honored, of course, Madame, but really —
CLARISSE: In the name of Christian charity!
HIMMELFAAHRT: I would like to oblige, but I must confess I am somewhat out of practice…
VENTROUX: *(Taking her by the arm and spinning her around.)* Are you quite finished?
CLARISSE: *(Backing her way towards HIMMELFAAHRT to perform the service.)* Please…please…
VENTROUX: Enough of these obscene displays. If you really want it, go do it yourself!
CLARISSE: *(Her voice breaking.)* But how can I?—I'd have to be double-jointed.
VENTROUX: Put on a compress or a bandage and stop carrying on!
CLARISSE: *(Clenching her fingers as if to scratch out her husband's eyes.)* Oh just go away—go away! If I die, on your conscience be it!
VENTROUX: Fine, fine.
CLARISSE: Oh the callousness of husbands! The cruelty of marriage!—*(Turns and screeches.)* Victor! Victor! *(She dashes out holding her backside.)* *(VENTROUX, exhausted, slumps into a chair.)*

VENTROUX: That woman will be the death of me.
HIMMELFAAHRT: *(After a moment's hesitation.)* M'sieur Ventroux…*(VENTROUX

turns towards HIMMELFAAHRT.) I hope you will forgive me, but I didn't feel it was my place to..

VENTROUX: Of course…of course…

HIMMELFAAHRT: I try not to fail in my duty to the fairer sex and I like to feel chivalry is still very much alive in our country, but we are barely acquainted…

VENTROUX: Naturally…naturally—think nothing of it.

HIMMELFAAHRT: And to provide such a service, necessary as it might be for Madame's health and well-being, seemed somewhat too forward—especially as I am a bachelor.

VENTROUX: Don't fret your head about it Himmelfaahrt. No one can blame you for declining to suck my wife.

HIMMELFAAHRT: I am pleased we share a mature understanding of the situation.

VENTROUX: Perfectly…perfectly.

(CLARISSE bursts back into the room with a shame-faced VICTOR following hard upon.)

CLARISSE: You're all cowards, the whole lot of you! Including Victor!

VENTROUX: What now?

CLARISSE: He wouldn't suck either.

VICTOR: *(Sheepishly.)* I didn't think it was my place, sir.

VENTROUX: Good God woman, are you going to everyone in the neighborhood and ask them to suck you?

CLARISSE: The pain is excruciating. I can feel the infection bubbling in my bloodstream.

VENTROUX: Then go to a doctor.

CLARISSE: *(A sudden realization.)* Right! There's a doctor on the floor above. Why didn't I think of that?

VENTROUX: He's not a doctor. He is a clerk at the Health Ministry. He has no license to practice.

CLARISSE: I don't care. He must know *something* about medicine if he works at the Health Ministry. Go and get him, Victor. Bring him down immediately.

VICTOR: At once, ma'am.

CLARISSE: *(Rubbing her backside and examining her hand.)* I need a compress…or a poultice…or a sling.

VENTROUX: You'll have your work cut out for yourself putting that into a sling. *(CLARISSE dashes back into her room.)*

VICTOR: *(Fearfully approaching VENTROUX.)* Sir, I hope you're not angry with me for not having…you know, Madame. I didn't think it was my place.

VENTROUX: *(Not wanting to discuss it.)* Yes…yes…yes…

VICTOR: I try to serve Madame in every way I can. I am *devoted* to Madame, but this seemed to me to be beyond the call of duty.

HIMMELFAAHRT: *(Putting his arm around VICTOR.)* I know just how you feel, old fellow. There are some things that are beyond the pale.

VICTOR: Exactly, sir. You understand, don't you.

HIMMELFAAHRT: Perfectly. *(They embrace and commune for a moment.)*

VICTOR: *(Turning back to VENTROUX.)* If, on the other hand, you feel this does lie within the scope of my duties, I would certainly try to…

VENTROUX: *(Irate.)* Would you just go and get the Health Official from upstairs!

VICTOR: Certainly, M'sieur. *(Rushing towards the door; stops and turns.)* I like to feel there is no sacrifice so great that I would not make —

VENTROUX: Get out will you before I throw a plate at your head!

(VICTOR exits hurriedly almost running into JAIVAL, who is just about to knock. JAIVAL is a cocky little man with a camera strapped around his shoulder.)

JAIVAL: I see you are quick off the mark here in admitting visitors.

VICTOR: M'sieur?

JAIVAL: M'sieur Ventroux?

VENTROUX: I am Ventroux. What do you want?

JAIVAL: *(Entering rapidly and coming straight up to VENTROUX, almost nose-to-nose.)* M'sieur Ventroux. I am Romain de Jaival from Le Figaro.

VENTROUX: Go on Victor,—upstairs! *(VICTOR hurries out.)* What can I do for you?

JAIVAL: I have been sent by my paper to interview you, M'sieur Ventroux. They would like an in-depth piece, with accompanying photos, both amusing and informative and brilliantly composed, and so naturally, they sent me.

VENTROUX: Ah ha.

JAIVAL: On political questions mainly…Your last few speeches have placed you squarely in the public eye.

VENTROUX: *(Flattered.)* Have they now?

JAIVAL: I am only expressing what has become general knowledge. There is great interest in your ideas, particularly your most recent proposal about birth control among the farm workers, state-sponsored midwives and a special tax on unwed mothers.

VENTROUX: Ah yes, a pet project of mine and one that I have very much taken to heart.

JAIVAL: The thing is I would like to do something fresh and original with this story. I am well known for turning out provocative, and if I do say so myself, astonishing columns. I write daily, as you may know. Perhaps you are familiar with my by line?

VENTROUX: Yes, of course, of course…M'sieur…um…?

JAIVAL: Jaival. Romain de Jaival of the Normandy Jaivals. My father was the first to publish a paper entirely in red ink. You may recall the publication—Les Toutes Rouge. It was suspended when they found the ink was toxic, irremovable and caused septicemia.

VENTROUX: Yes, I remember something of that. There were two or three fatalities, I believe.

JAIVAL: *(Solemnly.)* All martyrs to the cause of Journalism. A red hand became a mark of distinction among the press. I wear it myself. *(Shows a dark red smudge mark on the palm of his hand.)*

VENTROUX: Well, I'm at your disposal, M'sieur Jaival—although there is a small matter to which I must first attend. *(Introducing him.)* M'sieur Himmelfaahrt.

JAIVAL: No stranger to me or my publication. The Mayor of Moussilon-les-Indrets, I believe. I am delighted to make your acquaintance, M'sieur Himmelfaahrt.

HIMMELFAAHRT: Himmel*faahr*.

JAIVAL: Just so. I have visited your town on two or three occasions. The last time was just a few months back when the Paris Express suddenly got derailed there on the way to Morinville.

HIMMELFAAHRT: Yes, many travelers are first introduced to the beauties of our little community town in that way.

VENTROUX: If you'd be so good as to wait for a moment while the Mayor and I convene in the study. In five minutes, I shall be at your disposal.

JAIVAL: Don't mind me, M'sieur. If I may, I will just sit at this table and make a few notes while I am waiting.

VENTROUX: By all means, M'sieur. Come along, M'sieur le Mayor.

HIMMELFAAHRT: Lead on, M'sieur le Ministere.

(They exit into the study.)

(JAIVAL, strutting like a peacock, circles the room, taking stock of the sur-

roundings, the paintings, the decorations etc. He then takes out his camera and snaps a few "atmospheric shots" of the politician's chamber to accompany his story.)

CLARISSE: *(Bounding in from off-stage, still in her transparent nightie.)* Has he come down yet? What's taking him so long?

JAIVAL: *(Emitting a small cry of astonishment at the sudden appearance of CLARISSE in her nightie.)* Aghhh!!!

CLARISSE: *(Discovering JAIVAL.)* Ah, at last. I thought you would never get here. *(Pulling him up by the hand and turning her backside to him.)* Hurry Doctor and take a look.

JAIVAL: *(Shocked.)* At what Madame?

CLARISSE: Where I was stung.

JAIVAL: Stung, Madame?

CLARISSE: *(Pulling up the blind.)* Here, I'll pull up the blind so you can get a good look.

JAIVAL: A good look at what, Madame?

CLARISSE: You'll see it at once, Doctor.

JAIVAL: Excuse me, Madame. But I am no Doctor.

CLARISSE: Yes, I know you're not licensed, but that doesn't matter a bit. Here, take a look.

(Bends over and pulls up her gown.)

JAIVAL: *(Dazzled by the sight.)* Oh, my God!

CLARISSE: Is it that serious, M'sieur? Tell me the truth. Can you see it? Can you see it?

JAIVAL: Quite, quite clearly!

CLARISSE: Well, what do you think? — Please, spare me nothing.

JAIVAL: *(To himself.)* Pink, curvatious and succulent, Madame. *(Aside.)* This column will fetch me the Prix de Goncourt.

CLARISSE: What do you say?

JAIVAL: May I take a few notes?

CLARISSE: There's no time for that. Here, touch it.

JAIVAL: *(Beat.)* You want me to…

CLARISSE: Touch it and you'll see exactly what I'm talking about.

JAIVAL: *(Beat.)* If you insist, Madame. *(He touches the right side of her ass.)*

CLARISSE: Not there—on the other side!

(He touches the other side of her ass.)

CLARISSE: *(Worried.)* Well, what do you think, Doctor?

JAIVAL: *(The connoisseur.)* Mag-ni-fique, Madame!

CLARISSE: What are you talking about? Can you see the wasp sting? I'm sure it's still in there.

JAIVAL: You think so?

CLARISSE: Well, take a look!

JAIVAL: *(Trying to adjust to the situation.)* As you wish, Madame. *(He puts on his monocle and crouches down.)*

CLARISSE: Do you see it; do you see it?

JAIVAL: Yes, yes—there it is.

CLARISSE: I knew it; I knew it.

JAIVAL: It's just barely protruding…If I use my fingernails…

CLARISSE: Oh, give it a try doctor. Give it a try.

JAIVAL: I'll do my best, Madame.

(HIMMELFAAHRT and VENTROUX emerge from the study, take in the bizarre scene and are flabbergasted. VENTROUX forces HIMMELFAAHRT to make an about-turn.)

CLARISSE: *(Perfectly calm and not changing position.)* Please don't disturb us now. We've only just got started.

JAIVAL: *(The sting between his fingers.)* I have it, Madame. Here is the little sucker. *(Holding it up triumphantly.)*

(VENTROUX pounces on JAIVAL and sends him sprawling across the room. CLARISSE straightens up and turns to her husband).

CLARISSE: What is the matter with you?

VENTROUX: *You are showing your derriere to a writer from* Le Figaro?!?

CLARISSE: Le Figaro?

VENTROUX: To Romain de Jaival from Le Figaro!

CLARISSE: *(Dashing over to the fallen journalist and in a frantic tone of voice.)* Romain de Jaival.—*You* are Romain de Jaival. *(Sudden change of attitude.)* What a hilarious column you had in yesterday's paper. *(To VENTROUX.)* Did you see it, Julien? It was absolutely priceless.

VENTROUX: *(Throwing his arms up to the heavens.)* I am cursed!—Damned! — A plaything of the Gods!!! *(Suddenly realizes the blinds have been taken down from the window leaving the room entirely exposed. He lets out a bloodcurdling scream and rushes to the window.)* Aghhhhhh! Clemenceau! Clemenceau!

HIMMELFAAHRT: *(Aside to JAIVAL.)* It's another attack.

VENTROUX: Clemenceau!

STARK NAKED • 33

CLARISSE: Where? *(At window.)* Oh, you're right. *(Smiles and waves out the window.)* Bonjour M'sieur Clemenceau…ça va?

VENTROUX: *(Beside himself.)* He's laughing…sniggering…in stitches. *(Falls onto the sofa.)* I'm ruined. My political career is over!

CLARISSE: *(Out the window, waving cheerily.)* Allo, M'sieur Clemenceau.—Ça va bien??—

(As HIMMELFAAHRT stands frozen in terror, JAIVAL takes out his camera and snaps a picture of the fallen VENTROUX then CLARISSE then VENTROUX and then again CLARISSE, recording the scene for posterity and the front pages of LE FIGARO as the curtain falls.)

END OF PLAY

Henry Becque's
La Parisienne

Translated and Freely Adapted
by Charles Marowitz

CAST OF CHARACTERS

LAFONT
CLOTILDE
DU MESNIL
ADELE
SIMPSON

ACT ONE

An elegant drawing room. Double doors at the rear and at the side. A slim and expensive-looking writing desk. Center table with large blotter on it. Divan, armchairs, mirrors, flowers, etc.

At Rise, the stage is empty. CLOTILDE enters from the rear doors. She is fashionably dressed—gloves, hat, etc.—obviously just arrived from outside. She takes the letter she is holding over to the center table and hides it under the blotter then takes a batch of keys out of her pocket and moves to the writing desk. LAFONT enters and espies her at the desk. CLOTILDE pretends to be locking the desk. LAFONT bears down on her, palpably smouldering with rage.

LAFONT: Open that desk and give me that letter!

CLOTILDE: I beg your pardon!

LAFONT: Open that desk and give me that letter!

CLOTILDE: I will *not!*
    (Pause as LAFONT smoulders and searches for another ploy.)

LAFONT: Where have you been?

CLOTILDE: Ah, a different tack.

LAFONT: Yes, a different tack. Where have you been?

CLOTILDE:*(Nonchalantly.)* Pardon?

LAFONT: *(Bubbling over.)* I said where have you—

CLOTILDE: I wish you could just see yourself—like Vesuvius spouting lava. What a terrible face. I far prefer the one you wore yesterday. What are we coming to when a harmless little note that could've been penned by virtually anyone causes such an uproar?

LAFONT: Open that desk and give me that letter!

CLOTILDE: Back to that again?

LAFONT: Open that desk and—

CLOTILDE: Have it your way, but you'd better know that if you carry on like this, things are going to come to a screeching halt between us. I'm warning you. I'm not going to be interrogated every time I set foot outside the door.

LAFONT: Where have you been?

CLOTILDE: Haven't heard that one for a while.

LAFONT: Where have you—

CLOTILDE: Now be reasonable for God's sake. If I *had* just been with somebody does it seem logical he'd write me a note before I even got home?

LAFONT: Open that desk and give me that letter!

CLOTILDE: You're like a stuck phonograph record! —Or are you joking?

LAFONT: Do I look like I'm joking?

CLOTILDE: You're really accusing me then?

(LAFONT points sternly and impatiently toward the desk.)

CLOTILDE: So you insist! You demand! You issue orders! All right then, so be it.

(For the sake of appearances, she fumbles around in the pocket of her dress, finds a handkerchief, then a compact, then the keys which she throws at him. LAFONT ducks judiciously and they clatter at his feet.)

CLOTILDE: Open it yourself!

(LAFONT, thrown off guard, stands motionless looking at the desk, then at CLOTILDE then back at the desk.)

CLOTILDE: You're the one that's so curious. Pick them up. Open it! Be a man, for God's sake. If you start something, bloody well finish it.

(After a moment of tremulous hesitation, LAFONT stoops and picks up the keys. As soon as he does so, CLOTILDE turns on him.)

CLOTILDE: Best be warned. If you touch those keys, even with the tippy-tiniest-tips of your fingers, you'll be sorry.—You! Not I!

(LAFONT hesitates for a moment, then hands the keys to CLOTILDE.)

LAFONT: Take your keys.

(After a beat, CLOTILDE calmly removes her hat and gloves and, the tension gone, spreads herself on the divan.)

CLOTILDE: It's getting out of hand, you know.

LAFONT: What is?

CLOTILDE: You are. Your lunacy.

LAFONT: My—?

CLOTILDE: I know very well you've been clocking me left and right, coming and going, and I've said nothing. It was jealousy, of course, but quite flattering to a woman's vanity. Even somewhat amusing. But now it's turned into something else. Something stupid and crude and tawdry and it isn't in the *least* amusing. That kind of jealousy is unforgivable.—Do you promise to stop it?

LAFONT: *(Weakening.)* Clotilde.

CLOTILDE: Do you swear?

LAFONT: I promise.

CLOTILDE: But do you *swear?*

LAFONT: I swear!

CLOTILDE: That's a good boy.

LAFONT: *(Amorously.)* Clotilde…

CLOTILDE: What is it now, darling?

LAFONT: Do you love me?

CLOTILDE: Not as much as I did yesterday.

LAFONT: You want me to be happy?

CLOTILDE: Don't be silly, darling.

LAFONT: I can't bear the sight of all those men swarming around you.

CLOTILDE: Don't be an ass. I talk to this one and that one, but once they're gone, it's as if they were never there. I don't even remember their names.

LAFONT: But was there one particular one that you…encouraged? Who thought he could go further…

CLOTILDE: *(Mock shock.)* Go further?

LAFONT: One that you singled out from all the others?

CLOTILDE: Not one.

LAFONT: Who felt he had in some way, touched you, impressed you—*(Abruptly pleading tearfully.)* Open that desk and give me that letter!!!

CLOTILDE: Oh, not again!—That letter is from my friend, Mrs. Doyen-Beaulieu—one of the most proper women in France, despite all inferences to the contrary. It's perfectly harmless and I shall be glad to convey its contents to you, as you soon as you stop badgering me.

LAFONT: *(Softening.)* Clotilde.

CLOTILDE: *(Controlling her ire.)* Yes, darling.

LAFONT: Are you a reasonable woman?

CLOTILDE: I like to think so.

LAFONT: Is your mind easy?

CLOTILDE: I'm easy all over.

LAFONT: Think of me, Clotilde and think of yourself. Remember what's done cannot be undone. Don't yield to these terrible temptations that claim so many victims today. Resist it, Clotilde, resist it! So long as you are faithful to me, you remain pure and respectable, but the moment you deceive me… *(CLOTILDE puts a finger to her lips shushing LAFONT, then turns apprehensively towards the rear door.)*

CLOTILDE: Look out, it's my husband!

(DU MESNIL, suave, dressed in sober stripes, enters from the rear doors.)

DU MESNIL: I thought I heard your voice, Lafont. Lord, how you two carry on together—chattering and gossiping. Even an earthquake wouldn't stop you.

CLOTILDE: So you're back?

DU MESNIL: Yes, quite a while now.

CLOTILDE: Oh, how long a while?

DU MESNIL: A good while now.

CLOTILDE: How rude of you to skulk away in corners instead of entertaining our guest.

DU MESNIL: I was just tidying up a few things upstairs.

CLOTILDE: And what did Uncle have to say?

DU MESNIL: Never got to see him.

CLOTILDE: Is he always as elusive as that?

DU MESNIL: He asked me to pop back later today.

CLOTILDE: Shall I accompany you?

DU MESNIL: You'd only be in the way.

CLOTILDE: *(Bitchily.)* Thanks very much.

DU MESNIL: *(Putting his arm around LAFONT's shoulder.)* How are you, old man? Good to see you. Making out all right?

LAFONT: *(Squirmy.)* As well as can be expected.—And you?

DU MESNIL: In a foul mood, Lafont. Absolutely foul.

LAFONT: Anything I can do?

DU MESNIL: I work like a slave—all hours of the day—it's killing me.

LAFONT: You need a long vacation.

DU MESNIL: You need time and money for that.

LAFONT: You do all right, Du Mesnil.

DU MESNIL: I make it with one hand and spend it with the other.

LAFONT: Ambidextrous.

DU MESNIL: Ey?

LAFONT: I mean, that must be quite jolly—earning and spending.

DU MESNIL: Jolly? When you're young and carferee perhaps. But when you've responsibilities…

CLOTILDE: Stop whining, Du Mesnil, do you imagine Lafont is in any way interested in listening to your complaints. Or I, for that matter. What good does it do? Your appetite's fine. You sleep well. And you're probably the most pampered husband in Paris. You work—of course you work—everybody works. If I were in your place, I'd do five times as much as you do, and you wouldn't hear a peep out of me.

DU MESNIL: She's a marvel, Lafont; a veritable marvel. But you've no idea what a household this is. Every year, the costs go up and every day, there's some expensive little item or other that we just have to have.

CLOTILDE: You do go on, Adolph.

DU MESNIL: Let me get a word in edgeways, my dear. You were both gabbing away to beat the band. If you claim to be so industrious, why don't you sew up the boy's trousers. He's beginning to look like a little urchin. As if a gaggle of alley cats have been at the seat of his pants.

CLOTILDE: I don't think alley cats come in a "gaggle." —Besides the boy's spoiled rotten.

DU MESNIL: Why don't you take a needle and thread to his clothes?

CLOTILDE: That's why we have a chambermaid, darling.

DU MESNIL: *(To LAFONT.)* We're trying to live as thriftily as we can, but things pile up. You can't fob off servants with a few centimes anymore. We used to just give them gratuities—now they want annuities. The wife needs to be dressed fashionably of course, and so whatever we save on the house is spent in the shops. We eat out most of the time. In fact I can't remember what my own dining room looks like any more. That costs, but then I must admit, it beats home cooking.

CLOTILDE: Then what are you complaining about?

DU MESNIL: It's true I'd rather have haute cuisine outside then burnt offerings at home.

CLOTILDE:*(Getting peeved.)* Enough now. Let's talk about cheerier things.

DU MESNIL: You've got the right idea, Lafont. The Bachelor-Life! Don't ever change your lot!

LAFONT: Do *you* agree, Madame Du Mesnil?

CLOTILDE: Married, unmarried—I don't see the difference myself. *(She moves away to mix herself a drink.)*

DU MESNIL: You're more tolerant than my wife, Lafont. You'll listen to my complaints, won't you?

LAFONT: With pleasure.

DU MESNIL: At the moment, there are some people working on my behalf who might, well…change my situation.

LAFONT: How do you mean?

DU MESNIL: My uncle, you know, Jean-Baptiste, he's a member of the Academy and for a long time now, he's been unhappy about my position. He'd like to see me in the Treasury Department. He's got quite a few friends there and, little by little, they've been pulling a few strings.

LAFONT: Ah, perfect. I can just see it. You'd be your own man; you wouldn't have to answer to anyone.

DU MESNIL: I'm doing quite well at the Farm Board, you know. I've moved from pork bellies into harvesting and manure. I write regularly for their monthly bulletin. A few weeks back I caused a sensation with my article on innoculating chickens against the chicken pox.

LAFONT: Do chickens *get* the chicken pox?

DU MESNIL: No, thats why it caused it such a sensation. My name is on everyone's lips there. But Jean-Baptiste doesn't approve. He thinks I'm made for higher things and now that I have a wife and a child, I should find a more exalted postion.

LAFONT: I totally agree.

DU MESNIL: I'm not a scientist or a statistician—that's not me. I'm really more of an intellectual, I suppose. Did you ever read my paper on "The Metaphysical Implications Of Pork Belly Farming."

LAFONT: No, I don't think I—

DU MESNIL: "The Psychosomatic Origins of Foot-and-Mouth Disease"?

LAFONT: I'm afraid I never—

DU MESNIL: They're not for the masses, of course; they're not potboilers. Very much for a select miniority. To date, both combined have sold one hundred and nineteen copies—one hundred and *eighteen* really—one was eaten by a parrot at the last county fair. Terrible incident actually; believe the bird choked to death shortly afterward. Nothing to do with the content, of course; the newsprint didn't agree with it, or something.—I sort of visualize a whole new field for myself where I could really come into my own.

LAFONT: Get that Treasury job first. Then you can branch out and do whatever you like.— I'll see what *I* can do.

DU MESNIL: Don't interfere, Lafont, I beg you. My uncle, Jean-Baptiste, has got the matter well in hand. It seems to me when a distinguished member of the Academy agrees to do a favor, and when that favor is for his favorite nephew, and when that nephew is already a "coming man" as it were—papers, pamphlets, bulletins, that kind've thing—the government has no option but to grant it, wouldn't you say?

LAFONT: Good government jobs don't grow on trees.

DU MESNIL: This one is ripe for the plucking, Lafont; I can assure you.

LAFONT: Tell me, is the posting in Paris?

DU MESNIL: In Paris of course. My wife wouldn't dream of living in the country.
(During the last exchange, CLOTILDE has been seated at the desk, taunting LAFONT with the letter, brandishing it at him without her husband seeing. This business should coincide with DU MESNIL's last speech.)

CLOTILDE: *(Rising.)* Adolph, read this letter.

DU MESNIL: Who's it from?

CLOTILDE: Open it and see.
(Defiantly hands him the letter, very much for LAFONT'S benefit.)

DU MESNIL: It's from Pauline. "My dear Clotilde, you will shortly be receiving, if you haven't already, an invitation to Mrs. Simpson's grand ball on the

25th. It's all highly respectable. I dropped your name, Mrs. Simpson caught it, remarking that she remembered you very well, that you were an utterly charming person and she would be delighted to have you attend.—So you are now part of the "inner circle" and I'm sure you and Mrs. Simpson will get on famously together. She's not as young as she used to be. You must tell me how old you think she is, and I'll shock you by telling you how old she *really* is. Still, when she's all decked out for the ball, décolleté, diamonds and face-paint, though no longer quite a queen, she is still intimidatingly regal. But it's all a front. She's really something of a wild card. Extremely permissive and frolicosme. There is no indiscretion, no matter how scandalous, that she doesn't excuse. A true aristocrat."

"A wild card"…"frolicsome"…"no indiscretion, no matter how scandalous"…I can't say I'm much impressed with your "Mrs. Simpson."

LAFONT: Your friend sounds decidedly flighty, Madame Du Mesnil.

DU MESNIL: I've heard of this "Mrs. Simpson," now that I recall. There have been some rather shady stories circulating about her in the City.

LAFONT: Her reputation is deplorable.

DU MESNIL: I'll not take you into that woman's house, Clotilde.

LAFONT: I assure you madame, it is not a place for you. Filled as it is, with people of dubious reputation.

DU MESNIL: It must strike you that Lafont and I are of exactly the same mind in regard to this woman.

CLOTILDE: Very well. As you wish. If we don't go to Mrs. Simpson's ball, we'll go somewhere else. *(Turning to DU MESNIL.)* But in future, I would hope you would wait until we are alone and in private before discussing such matters. I'm not accustomed to having my social life decided by strangers. *(She turns away angrily.)*

DU MESNIL: What are you saying? Lafont, a stranger? *(To LAFONT.)* Have you two had a tiff?

LAFONT: It's you Adolph. You're the one who's got on her nerves.

DU MESNIL: *(To CLOTILDE.)* Well, I'm off.

CLOTILDE: *(Coldly.)* Bye-bye.

DU MESNIL: What are you going to do?

CLOTILDE: Whatever I please.

DU MESNIL: Where are we dining tonight?

CLOTILDE: I don't know and couldn't care less.

DU MESNIL: Is that a way to talk?

CLOTILDE: It is when talking to a quarrelsome, disagreeable man.

DU MESNIL: Are you saying you *want* to go this ball?

CLOTILDE: The ball is neither here nor there. I've already forgotten all about it. I'm not a moonstruck teenager you know, who gets all ga-ga about "going to a ball." But you—you complain, you whine, you trample on your wife's feelings with great hobnail boots. Anyone listening to you would have a very low opinion of our married life.

DU MESNIL: You mustn't take all that so seriously, Clotilde. That's the way all husbands carry on. They growl and bark and put down their foot, but when the air's cleared, you always get exactly what you want. You know very well you wear the pants in this family. *(Clotilde smiles.)* Wouldn't you agree, Lafont?

LAFONT: *(Beat.)* I have no opinion about your wife's under garments.

DU MESNIL: I'm just very churned up about this job at the Treasury Department. It would mean a lot to us if I actually got it. What do you think Clotilde, I mean objectively speaking; do you think I have a chance?

CLOTILDE: Time will tell.

DU MESNIL: I have excellent qualifications, years of experience, and when called upon, I can certainly exude authority.

CLOTILDE: You certainly do exude, Adolph.

DU MESNIL: And I've got the backing of lots of competent men.

CLOTILDE: With virtually no influence.

DU MESNIL: But what about Jean-Baptiste and the weight of the French Academy?

CLOTILDE: A lot of waxworks, Adolph—you know that very well.

DU MESNIL: Waxworks?—My uncle?—Jean-Baptiste?

CLOTILDE: You're making a big mistake in keeping me out of this whole business.

DU MESNIL: You?—What could you do?

CLOTILDE: A thousand things that only a woman *can* do as she goes on her merry little rounds. I'd put all my spies to work—starting with Pauline. She quite admires you—I could never understand why—And Pauline is hand-in-glove with Mrs. Simpson who is very well connected in political circles. When you so blithely dismiss the idea of visiting Mrs. Simpson, you really make me laugh. As if she gives a tinker's damn whether we show up or not. Every evening, the most influential people in Paris are to be found at her salon. Diplomats, ministers, ambassadors. If you were at dinner with them—on equal terms —you could expound your brilliant ideas while you puffed those hideous black cigars you're so fond of. And when the smoke cleared and those dreary officials came to you and said: "We're sorry but the job is now spoken for," you could turn 'round and say: "I know; I've got the appointment in my pocket." That's the way I would conduct this business, but then, I'm only a woman.—What do I know?

DU MESNIL: *(After a moment of reflection.)* You may be right If my uncle can't swing this thing with his contacts, we'll try your way. Woman's intuition and all that.

CLOTILDE: What would men's incompetence do without it?

DU MESNIL: You may have a point.

CLOTILDE: One of us ought to. *(Intimately to him.)* Anyway, you know I can be irresistible when I want to be. *(She smiles then CLOTILDE and DU MESNIL laugh together.)*

DU MESNIL: I'm off to see Uncle. Shall I take along Lafont or are you keeping him with you?

CLOTILDE: Leave him here. He irritates me, but amuses me as well. *(Whispering to her husband.)* It's his nose, I think. I can't look at it without giggling.

DU MESNIL: *(Whispering.)* You are a brute to Lafont and he is always so kind and obliging.

CLOTILDE: *(Whispering.)* I'd hate to be kissed by a nose like that. It would positively have me in stitches. *(They both share a laugh.)*

DU MESNIL: Well, I'm off. *(Turning to LAFONT.)* You'd better stay here if I'm really as great an ogre as my wife says. *(Confidentially.)* You've no idea what it is to have a wife and family. One loves them, of course, provides for them, thinks about them all the time, but sometimes one just wishes they'd all just disappear. *(Then brightly to CLOTILDE.)* Bye, bye darling. *(He Exits.)*

CLOTILDE: *(Dropping her mask.)* Do you see now how careful we have to be!—If he'd come in one minute earlier, we'd've both been lost.

LAFONT: *(Back on his high horse.)* You made a fool of me!

CLOTILDE: *(Confused.)* When was that?

LAFONT: With that letter. Why didn't you just show it to me when I asked you!?

CLOTILDE: *(Amused.)* I knew you wouldn't like it, and I was right. Besides, I used it simply as bait. To see how far you'd actually go.

LAFONT: You were being cruel.

CLOTILDE: You were being stupid.—Now I'm going to set your mind at ease, although God knows you don't deserve it. The fact is my husband reads all my mail—every single letter—without exception. I wouldn't have it any other way. How else could he be assured of my complete fidelity?—Now let's sit down and talk this out without losing our tempers. First, you in a rage, and then him in a sulk—it's really too much for one day. How can you possibly justify your outrageous behavior? Where is all this absurd jealousy leading?

It all started—quite suddenly—around January 15th.—I have good reason for remembering that date.

LAFONT: And that is…?

CLOTILDE: None of your business. Are you going to question every word I say? We might as well be in the divorce court. Now let's be calm and reasonable. Go'head. Have your say.

(LAFONT, *suddenly being given the floor, is slightly flummoxed. He rises imperiously, reflects for a moment, is about to speak; thinks better of it; reflects again, then blurts out.*)

LAFONT: Where have you been?

CLOTILDE:*(Suppressing her laughter.)* That's right; that's right. You did ask that several times before and never got an answer.—Right.—The fact is I had an appointment. *(LAFONT rises and begins to fume.)* With my milliner! In her boutique. Not exactly a den of inquity with half-naked men draped around the shelves. You *will* allow me to visit with my milliner, I hope. Now how does that in any way wrong you. I simply can't understand.

LAFONT:*(His anger segueing into self-pity.)* I barely see you at all these days.

CLOTILDE: Poppycock! What are you doing now? Am I not? If you want to waste time quarelling instead of spending the time more agreeably, that's your loss.

LAFONT: *(The hurt child—holding back tears.)* I waited for you all this week…last week too, and the week before that.

CLOTILDE: Fiddlesticks. And even if it were true, if I broke every promise I every made to you, not once but a thousand times, is that any reason to think the worst of me? Am I free to do as I please? Am I not dependent on everyone in this house. I am married you know.—No, there must be something else. Come on, out with it!

LAFONT: *(Pause then taking the bit in his teeth.)* It seems to me that you are cooling…

CLOTILDE: Cooling?

LAFONT: Lacking a certain warmth…

CLOTILDE: You make me sound like a ventilation system.

LAFONT: That you no longer care about our relationship, that you're seeking novelty—indeed, may already have found it…that we're at that inevitable stage in a relationship where little white lies begin to appear, and bad faith, and shabby behavior and indignities.

CLOTILDE: I've no idea when things like that start in a relationship. It would seem you are more experienced in such matters than I am. I'm asking for facts—clear and unambiguous facts—which I can refute with facts of my own. I can't deal with your fantasies—those sordid little demons running around in your warped imagination.

LAFONT: That date—January 15th—that you remember so exactly—

CLOTILDE: What about it?

LAFONT: It rings a bell with me as well.

CLOTILDE: Nonsense, it can't possibly mean anything to you.

LAFONT: I've noticed a number of little things.

CLOTILDE: What sort of things?

LAFONT: Lots of things.

CLOTILDE: Lots of what-things?

LAFONT: Small things.

CLOTILDE: How small?

LAFONT: Small, pertinent things — Oh, just little details of course, but what is it they say in the law courts: the devil is in the details.

CLOTILDE: You're losing me.

LAFONT: You've changed, Clotilde—without even noticing it, I suspect. For one thing, you're always making fun of me. I am the constant butt of your humor. You've become absent minded, and embarrassed about little things. It's as if you were constantly hiding things from me. And you're always contradicting yourself.

CLOTILDE:*(Slightly astonished.)* Fascinating—do go on.

LAFONT: You talk to me about people that live in a completely different world from ourselves, and you seem to know everything about their comings and goings. How is *that,* I wonder. And you seem to be up on all the latest scandals, dishing out the dirt on all and sundry whereas previously, it was I that was telling you all the current gossip. And your political opinions have utterly transformed.

CLOTILDE: What a child you are Lafont—and I'm just as bad for taking all this seriously.—My political opinions! You mean I'm a reactionary? Well you're right there, I *am* a reactionary and proud of it. I like law and order and old, established principles. I want the churches to be open every Sunday—in the unlikely event that I get the urge to drop into one. I want the shops to be open all hours of the day and chockfull of the prettiest and most expensive items—even if I can't afford them. I want all the hoodlums in the street to be sent to Devil's Island and if they're devoured by sharks while trying to escape, I say to the sharks "Bon appetite!" And if my "political opinions" as you call them, have veered somewhat right of center, it seems to me you're the last person to complain. You are proud to call yourself a "democrat"—which these days simply means you talk like a liberal and vote conservative.

I honestly believe you could take up with a mistress who had no religion at all. —What a repugnant thought. —What was my husband talking to you about?
LAFONT: About a position he hoped to be getting.
CLOTILDE: Were you interested?
LAFONT: Very much.
CLOTILDE: You say "very much" as if it meant "not at all." And how did Adolph strike you?
LAFONT: He seems to be as always.
CLOTILDE: Not tired or careworn?
LAFONT: No.
CLOTILDE: Never mind. I don't know why I should talk to you about my husband at all, given the low opinion you have of him. My point is this: You know Adolph is looking for a government position and when one is doing that, one must treat the government with some respect. Do you think I would jeopardize his chances by criticising the current administration—just when we're hoping they will bestow a favor? A man would do that, without flinching. Men are about as sensitive as tadpoles. A woman, never! She not only knows on which side her bread is buttered, but precisely how to spread the jam and marmalade.

Shall I tell you your trouble, Lafont? You are an egotist. Do you know what an egotist is? It's a person who, no matter how much they appear to be looking at other people, only ever see themselves. You thought by lashing out at me, you might pick up some tittle-tattle that you could use against me. Well there isn't any, and so you can't. But don't think I'll forget your little ruse. A woman may forgive a slight, but she never forgets it and because it's not forgotten, it's never really forgiven. —Do you understand?
LAFONT: No.
CLOTILDE: Don't play stupid, Lafont. You're far too thick for that. You must be good, patient, uncomplaining and content with what you get, and not ask for the moon. You must remember that I have a household to maintain, a family to keep and friends to entertain. Pleasure is for after-hours,—if one is not too exhausted. Remember that the slightest outburst at an inopportune moment might compromise me fatally. So understand once and for all: I don't ever again wish to find you skulking outside my door, waving your arms and breathing fire when I've just come back from a harmless little visit to my dressmaker.
(LAFONT *who has listened to all this like a cowed little child with his head bowed, suddenly looks up.*)

CLOTILDE: What is it now?

LAFONT: *(As before.)* Where have you been?

CLOTILDE: I just told you.

LAFONT: You said you were at your *milliner's*.

CLOTILDE: And my dressmaker's.

LAFONT: You never mentioned your dressmaker's.

CLOTILDE: I went to one and then the other.

LAFONT: You said you were at your *milliner's*.

CLOTILDE: It's time you left.

LAFONT: No!

CLOTILDE: Yes!

LAFONT: Later!

CLOTILDE: Right now!

LAFONT: What's the hurry?

CLOTILDE: *I'm* in no hurry.

LAFONT: Neither am I! I'll stay.

CLOTILDE: Out of the question! If my husband returns and finds you still here, he might become suspicious. Be reasonable, Lafont, and just say good-bye.

LAFONT:*(Smouldering.)* Clotilde?

CLOTILDE: What now?

LAFONT: *(Casually.)* I'm going home.

CLOTILDE: Good idea. Glad you thought of it.

LAFONT:*(Slyly.)* Do you know what time it is?

CLOTILDE: Approximately.

LAFONT: The day is still young.

CLOTILDE: And I'm feeling like I'm ready for the wheelchair.

LAFONT: My flat is ten minutes away.

CLOTILDE: How convenient for you.

LAFONT: All you need do is put on your hat and coat.

CLOTILDE: I *thought* that's what you were getting at.

LAFONT: What do you say?

CLOTILDE:*(Beat.)* It's the only good idea you've come up with all day. *(Intimately.)* You go ahead.

LAFONT: You'll come after.

CLOTILDE: Shortly.

LAFONT: How soon?

CLOTILDE: In a few minutes. Go on, go on.

LAFONT: You won't forget.

CLOTILDE: I promise.

LAFONT: Then, I'll go, but don't for—
(CLOTILDE kisses him perfunctorily on the mouth to shut him up.)
LAFONT: *(Longingly.)* Clotilde…
CLOTILDE: Au revoir.
> *(She ushers him out. He stops for a moment then goes. Clotilde rings for her maid.)*

ADELE: You rang, madame?
CLOTILDE: *(Peeling off her dress.)* Fetch my dressing gown and slippers. I'm going to bed.

END OF ACT ONE

ACT TWO

The scene is the same as Act One. A few days later. CLOTILDE is dressed and ready to go out. She inspects herself in the glass. Tries out various theatrical attitudes and gestures as if rehearsing responses for both her lover and her husband. Shocked—coy—earnest—repentant—smug. During this pantomime, ADELE enters unnoticed and watches with a rapt expression. CLOTILDE suddenly spies ADELE in the mirror, comes back to normal and proceeds as if nothing untoward has occurred.

CLOTILDE: Do I look all right, Adele?
ADELE: Yes, madame.
CLOTILDE: Just all right?
ADELE: Very all right, madame.
CLOTILDE: And the time…?
ADELE: Almost three o'clock, madame.
CLOTILDE: Is everything laid out for me?
ADELE: *(Referring to the table.)* All the usual things: keys, address book, lipstick, powder…
CLOTILDE: Bring them over.
ADELE: *(Doing so.)* Madame will not be returning today?
CLOTILDE: Possibly not.
ADELE: *(Same tune.)* Probably not.
CLOTILDE: Why "probably"?
ADELE: M'sieur Du Mesnil is dining with his Treasury friends. He wouldn't miss that for the world.
CLOTILDE: So what?
ADELE: I've noticed that on such occasions, madame usually passes the day with her old schoolmate from the convent—the one that M'sieur has never seen.
CLOTILDE: Have you been peeking through keyholes, Adele?
ADELE: Certainly not! Besides, the keyholes in this apartment have very small apertures, madame.
CLOTILDE: How do you know that?
ADELE: The concierge pointed them out to me when I was first engaged. It's just that I've caught a word here or there. I raise the point only because my wretched brother…
CLOTILDE: Your brother?
ADELE: You will recall madame, he suffers from…

LA PARISIENNE • 51

CLOTILDE: Oh yes, I remember. Arthritis, bronchitis, rheumatism, astigmatism—it's a wonder he's still alive.
ADELE: *(Sadly.)* Only barely, madame.
CLOTILDE: And you wish to go and minister to him.
ADELE: I am all he has, madame.
CLOTILDE: How terribly unfortunate. *(Catching herself.)* I mean, that he has no other relatives to nurse him.—All right, all right. Go on, go on.
ADELE: I thank you, madame. And my brother thanks you, madame. And were he alive, my father would thank you, madame. —Is there anything else?
CLOTILDE: Don't let the cook leave. She must be on hand when M'sieur Du Mesnil returns home.
ADELE: Of course, madame. Shall I call you a cab?
CLOTILDE: I'll find one en route.
ADELE: *(Following her to the door.)* Have a pleasant day, madame.
   (The doorbell rings. CLOTILDE stops in her tracks; so does ADELE. The bell rings again.)
ADELE: The bell, madame.
CLOTILDE: I'm not deaf, Adele. *(Retracing her steps. To herself.)* Three o'clock. He hasn't seen me for a while. He knows the Treasury dinner is today. I should have known he'd have a relapse. *(To ADELE as the bell rings again.)* See to the door. I am at home to no one.
ADELE: If it should be M'sieur Lafont, madame…
CLOTILDE: To no one, Adele. Without exceptions.
ADELE: Very good, madame.
CLOTILDE: And leave the door open a crack so I can hear who it is. Should it be someone for my husband, bring them in and I'll come out.
ADELE: I understand, madame.
   (The bell rings again—two and three times.)
ADELE: *(Under her breath.)* Ooh la, what a boor! *(She moves out to the door.)*
CLOTILDE: If I'd've been a little faster, I'd be on my way by now and not be bothered. *(Holds open the door and listens.)* It's him all right; I recognize his grunt. Never misses an opportunity. *(Voices are raised outside.)* That's right, wake up the whole neighborhood. He's asking where I am.—Oh, I don't believe it. She's letting him in. He's actually coming in.—Just when you want rid of them, they cling like leeches.
   (CLOTILDE hides behind a curtain as LAFONT and ADELE enter.)
LAFONT: All right, all right, calm down, my dear girl.
ADELE: Why won't you take my word for it, sir? You can see there's no one about.
LAFONT: I'll wait.

ADELE: Wait for whom? Both m'sieur and madame have gone out.

LAFONT: Together?

ADELE: He went out by himself—and so did she.

LAFONT: Did he say when he'd be back?

ADELE: All I know is that madame is not coming back. She'll be dining in town.

LAFONT: With M'sieur Du Mesnil?

ADELE: No sir, they are dining separately.

LAFONT: You just get on with your work. I'll leave a note here on the desk.

ADELE: As you please, sir. This is not my house; I cannot show you the door.

LAFONT: I know quite well where the door is. I've just come through it. — Go on, go on.

(ADELE huffs and puffs and exits grumbling obscenities to herself. LAFONT, unaware that CLOTILDE is behind the curtain, gives way to gloom and desperation.)

LAFONT: I've barged in. I've no idea why I've barged in. Probably put my foot in it again. I must calm down. Make up my mind that it's done with and act accordingly.

You can't keep a semi-respectable mistress in this town. The more respectable she is, the less chance you have of keeping her. I'll have it out with Clotilde once and for all and break with her for good.

Here I am looking for her this way and that, and there she is running hither and thither. What's the point? I know damn well she's become Mercier's mistress. It's as clear as the stupid nose on my face; that nose which she so enjoys tweaking. Well, her "tweaking days" are over. Probably cares as little for Mercier as she did for me. —Some consolation!

If Adolph were here, at least we could spend some time together. Play cards, or chat, or something. Whenever she makes me miserable, there's no one like Adolph to revive my spirits. When I think of his situation, I'm somewhat consoled to my own. His is far worse than mine, of course. She wrongs me at every turn. But she's wronging him as well. I can see exactly what he has to put up with. We're really both in the same boat, he and I.

Here I am, desolate, cast out by her, unfriended by him, sick at heart about a ridiculous situation which gets worse and worse the longer I'm in it. What a cross we men have to bear! Either bachelors or cuckolds.—What a bloody choice!!!

(CLOTILDE comes out of hiding and presents herself before LAFONT, who is so wrapped up in his own thoughts, he doesn't register her presence but continues muttering to himself. After a moment or two, her presence finally dawns on him.)

LAFONT: Clotilde, you here?

CLOTILDE: What's so strange about that? This *is* my house. What's strange is *your* being here—especially after you've been told in no uncertain terms, that I am not at home.

LAFONT: But you *are* at home!

CLOTILDE: Not to you!—So this is the way you repay my kindness. You keep inventing new ways of insulting me and I, like a fool, keep forgiving you.

LAFONT: It's all your fault.

CLOTILDE: Oh, don't start all that again. No more scenes. I've had enough "scenes" to fill the Comedie Francaise for ten seasons. Have you any possible reason or pretext for storming into my house again? Some irresistible discovery that you positively had to share with me?

LAFONT: *(After a confused moment.)* I thought…you were ill.

CLOTILDE: I'm not. I'm well. *(Using her hand to imitate a bird in flight.)* Fly away!

LAFONT: You're going out?

CLOTILDE: What does it look like? I'm not in the habit of parading around the house in my hat and coat.

LAFONT: Are you going now?

CLOTILDE: I'm late. You're making me later.

LAFONT: Let's not jump to any conclusions.

CLOTILDE: What the hell does that mean?

LAFONT: I thought we might have dinner together—if I'm still your old schoolmate?

CLOTILDE: There is no more "old schoolmate." She's fallen into a sewer, broken her neck and will be buried by the end of the week. I've come to the conclusion that these afternoon trysts at romantic hideaways are fraught with danger. They involve me in revolting lies, and I'll have no more of them.— *(Pause.)* Don't you think that's best?

LAFONT: Don't ask me what I think.

CLOTILDE: You resent what I've said.

LAFONT: I am steeled for every calamity and every disaster.

CLOTILDE: That's by far the best course. It will spare you all future disappointments, of which I fear there will be many.

LAFONT: Could we please sit down and discuss this thing like adults.

CLOTILDE: I haven't the time now. Come back tomorrow.

LAFONT: When I do, something else will come up and you'll put me off until the day *after* tomorrow and then the day after that.

CLOTILDE: It is very hard to make time to speak to insolent and disagreeable people.

LAFONT: It's loving you that makes me so unbearable.

CLOTILDE: *(Exasperated.)* Who would have thought love could be such a bore!

LAFONT: Oh it's easy for you to be cruel. What do you care? Here I am wallowing in despair night after night while you are gadding about.

CLOTILDE: Gadding about! What a beastly figure of speech to use towards a woman you supposedly love. Let's concede, for argument's sake, that I have grown somewhat cool towards you, do you really think you can win me back by clubbing me into submission? That produces exactly the opposite effect. A woman grows bored, angry and starts contemplating things that would otherwise never have popped into her head.

(LAFONT droops visibly and CLOTILDE deliberately tries a more sympathetic tack.)

CLOTILDE: *(Tenderly.)* Why don't you take a nice long trip somewhere. Six months on the Zambezi would do you a world of good. You'd come back a new man. Don't think I'd forget you. I'm not that kind of woman. When you return, you'll find me just the way I was before you left. Won't you consider it, Lafont, for my sake?

LAFONT: Six months...on the *Zambezi!*

CLOTILDE: Wherever you like, I just suggested that because the climate's so agreeable. What do you say, darling? For me.

(He smoulders and says nothing.)

CLOTILDE: Can't you contemplate a short period away even to please your mistress?—Even when she'd regard it as a true sign of your love for her?

LAFONT: *(Shuddering.)* The Zambezi!—It's full of cannibals and tsetse flies.

CLOTILDE: *(Losing her cool.)* Alaska then, the icebergs are goregeous this time of year!

LAFONT *(Back to the old drill.)* Where are you going!?

CLOTILDE: Is that all you can find to say to me?

LAFONT: Where are you going?

CLOTILDE: I was sure you'd ask that. I've been waiting for it from the moment you barged in.

LAFONT: Does the question embarrass you?

CLOTILDE: Not in the least. I know you'll be profoundly relieved when I tell you where I'm going. And what's to prevent me from saying "I'm going here" and then going someplace else?

LAFONT: I'd follow you.

CLOTILDE: Go ahead, follow me! A lot of good it's done you so far. You'd best beware, Lafont. I am fond of you—really fond of you and I make allowances for many things; your delicate condition, your jealousy, your lunacy, but don't believe you can take advantage of my good nature indefinfitely. *(Pointedly.)* I do whatever I choose to do, and it's nobody's business—but my husband's.

LAFONT: *(Screeching.)* You are deceiving me!

CLOTILDE: With whom? The butcher? The baker? The local Gendarmerie? Vague suspicions will get you nowhere. If you wish to accuse a woman, you must have proof, and once you have proof, a real man knows what he must do: leave or shut up!

LAFONT: *(Helplessly.)* Clotilde…

CLOTILDE: Tell me his name, if you know it! I'd be glad to know this alluring Don Juan who has totally captivated me without my knowledge. You are forcing me to tell you something I vowed I'd never say. *(Dramatizing.)* I've committed a terrible sin. I had a husband, a child, a cosy little home and foolishly, I wanted more. I wanted to have it all. Like all women, I fantasized an ideal existence in which I could fulfill my marital duties without relinquishing my pleasures. I wanted heaven and earth—all rolled in to one. And it's taken you to show me how impossible that dream actually was. Another kind of woman might have pulled it off, but for me, everything now lies in ruins. What's done is done. I know I have only myself to blame, but I can tell you, it is the first and last time that I ever seek happiness. *(She sinks into the armchair, pats her eyes gently with her handkerchief and has succeeded in bringing herself to the desired emotional state.)*

LAFONT: You're crying.

CLOTILDE: *(Tearfully.)* It will pass. It will pass.

LAFONT: *(After a moment of guilty contemplation.)* I am a beast.

CLOTILDE: *(Tearfully.)* You can't help it.

LAFONT: I was wrong.

CLOTILDE: *(With deep feeling.)* Very, very wrong!

LAFONT: I'm going.

CLOTILDE: *(Casually.)* That's probably best.

(He trudges away in a stupor of guilt, then comes back. As he goes, CLOTILDE looks relieved, but as soon as he returns, she automatically returns to her suffering state.)

LAFONT: Forget everything I said. I didn't mean a word of it. I don't really believe that you are deceiving me. You are too good, too honest. I know that deep down, you appreciate the love I feel for you. I thought you were waiting for me; that we'd have our usual little tryst, as we always do when you see your old schoolmate. When you said "No," it was like being kicked in the stomach by a mule. *(Pleading again.)* Where are you going? Paying calls, visiting friends. Must you go!? Call it off. Send a note; say your husband is ill. Give me this night—which has always been mine and for which I have been longing all week.

CLOTILDE: I'd like to, but I can't.

LAFONT: Why not?

CLOTILDE: They're coming for me with a cab to take me to the park.

LAFONT: But you were all dressed to go out.

CLOTILDE: No, I was just waiting to be collected.

LAFONT: Is it…that Mrs. Simpson?

CLOTILDE: *(Thankful for the cue.)* Yes, we arranged to dine together. What a funny little man you are. You take offence at everything; even things that should relieve you.

LAFONT: *(Beginning to boil gain.)* Mrs. Simpson.

CLOTILDE: I'd forgotten—you don't approve of her. You'd forbidden me to enter her house. It's a delightful house, you know, magnificently furnished, and really quite cosy. There may be a few trifling love affairs going on there—who's to say—but it's no different from any other house in Paris.

LAFONT: That woman's reputation is wallowing in the gutter.

CLOTILDE: So much the worse for those who've put it there. *(Back to her lecturing manner.)* When a man has been intimate with a woman, she ought to be treated as if she were sacred—yes, sacred! That's something you should commit to memory, Lafont. It will serve you well in all your future liaisons.

Here you are, smouldering again like a volcano about to spew lava. I wonder what other horrors you've got in store. Today, you've wounded me with the worst insult a man can give to a woman. What's next? What's to follow? Only violence, I expect. I hope you have enough self-control to avoid strangling me to death or blacking both my eyes.—Consider, my friend, wouldn't it be best to part now on good terms, rather than wake up and find your picture splattered over Le Figaro and condemned to death for a *crime passionelle.*

I'm releasing you in earnest now—for both our sakes. Your mind is easy now, isn't it? Your temper cooled. Whatever you may feel about Mrs. Simpson, you must admit you would rather I were with her than with…*(She thinks better of finishing her sentence.)* And when we're both a little calmer, we'll discuss your little six-month trip to the Congo and, who knows, I may bring you around to my point of view.

LAFONT: *(Having quietly assimilated all of CLOTILDE's tenderness.)* And tomorrow?

CLOTILDE: What?

LAFONT: And tomorrow?

CLOTILDE: Are you back to that again? Tomorrow! You want to meet up tomorrow!

Very well, Lafont. Tomorrow then. But just listen to me. You're calm and collected now. Almost normal. Don't spoil it the moment you get outside the door. If I should encounter you between now and tomorrow—in the park or on the boulevard—or anywhere at all, you will never set eyes on me again!

LAFONT: Tomorrow then?

CLOTILDE: *(After a moment's rumination.)* Tomorrow.

(LAFONT rises somewhat reborn, immediately becomes disconsolate again, manages to muster a meek smile and exits.)

CLOTILDE: Well, what else could I do? He's just a child; a pathetic, backward, brain-damaged child. I don't really mind when he gets riled up. I quite enjoy that sometimes. But when he starts bawling, it's just awful. *(Goes to the window.)*

I better make sure he's really gone before I go downstairs. Look at him. Trudging away slowly with his head down. That sad sack of potatoes. I'll have to visit him tomorrow, I suppose. Just to make sure he doesn't swallow iodine or something.

What's he doing now? He's stopped. Oh my God, he's coming back. He's coming back into the house. Can you believe it? The bastard, he's going to lie in wait for me. — I'll confront him. I'll let him know I'm on to his diabolical tricks.—Oh, how in heaven am I ever going to get out of here!?

(DU MESNIL enters from the rear door. He looks thoroughly discouraged. He throws his hat angrily on to the table and sits disconsolately.)

CLOTILDE: If it's not one, it's the other. —Adolph, what's the matter with you? *(Adolph remains inconsolable.)* Are you all right?

DU MESNIL: *(Bitterly.)* Leave me alone, will you?

CLOTILDE: What *is* the matter? Your face is so long, you might trip on it.— What's happened?

DU MESNIL: Don't make me feel any worse than I do. I'm not in the mood for chatter right now.

CLOTILDE: Will you tell me what's the matter?

DU MESNIL: You'll know it all soon enough.

CLOTILDE: Is it serious?

DU MESNIL: Very serious.

CLOTILDE: You're angry about something.

DU MESNIL: I've every reason to be.

CLOTILDE: You're not angry with me, I hope?

DU MESNIL: You? Why should I be angry with you?

CLOTILDE: Exactly.

DU MESNIL: Exactly what? — You're not making any sense. You were on the way out, weren't you? Well then, run along.— Where are you going anyway?

CLOTILDE: Shopping.

DU MESNIL: Naturally. Go and get yourself a sack full of clothes. It's exactly the thing to do.

CLOTILDE: I'm not going to budge until you tell me what's going on. *(Removes her hat and coat.)* I'm not leaving my husband when he's in such a miserable state. *(Sits.)* I'll just sit here and wait till he deigns to talk to his patient little wife.

DU MESNIL: *(Softening.)* You're a dear.

CLOTILDE: And you're a silly goose.—Out with it!

DU MESNIL: We're done for.

CLOTILDE: How so?

DU MESNIL: The Treasury job. Phhtt!

CLOTILDE:*(Inquiringly.)* Phhtt?

DU MESNIL:*(Tragically.)* Phhtt!

CLOTILDE: Is that all?—You get me into a state of quiet delirium just because a little job at the Treasury has fallen through? Really Adolph.—That's the way business is. Somebody loses; somebody wins. If you're the winner, you gloat. If you're not, you just put it out of your head and get on with things.

Did you think I was going to reproach you? What a goose you are!—Now brace up and wipe that forlorn look off your face. You'd think the entire Chamber of Deputies had gone up in smoke. Which, come to think of it, might be the best thing that could happen to it. What would you do if there was a real calamity? If you lost me, for instance. Now tell me, which one of us was right?—A fine guardian angel your uncle turned out to be! The great puller-of-strings! Nothing ever pleased him. Neither your writings, or your wife, or your way of life. And no sooner does he put his oar in than the whole boat capsizes. How did he ever get into the Academy anyway? —It must have been a clerical error.

DU MESNIL: There it is.

CLOTILDE: It's all settled, is it?

DU MESNIL: Almost.

CLOTILDE:What do you mean "almost." It's either settled or it isn't. —Has—the—appointment—been—made—or—not?

DU MESNIL: Not yet.

CLOTILDE: Then it's *not* settled.

DU MESNIL: The post is about to be assigned and I've been given to understand that I'm not getting it.

CLOTILDE: Now we're finally getting somewhere. Who *is* getting it?

DU MESNIL: Some mediocrity or other.

CLOTILDE: A married mediocrity?

DU MESNIL: What's that got to do with it?

CLOTILDE: Just answer the question?

DU MESNIL: Yes, a married mediocrity.

CLOTILDE: A young wife?

DU MESNIL: About your age.

CLOTILDE: Attractive?

DU MESNIL: Mmm, cute.

CLOTILDE: Accommodating?

DU MESNIL: So they say.

CLOTILDE: *(Vindictively, to herself.)* The little whore!

DU MESNIL: Are you trying to imply…

CLOTILDE: Imply!?

DU MESNIL: You're all wrong. Things don't happen that way in politics.

CLOTILDE: To sum it all up, nobody's yet got the job and, as usual, you're just throwing in the sponge.

DU MESNIL: All right, have it your way. But there's nothing to be done about it. *(After a moment's reflection, CLOTILDE rises and purposefully moves to the desk. Once there, she begins writing frantically. After watching her for a few moments, DU MESNIL wanders over.)*

DU MESNIL: What in heaven's name are you—

CLOTILDE: Don't interrupt.

DU MESNIL: Can we discuss this?

CLOTILDE: Not just now. I've got to finish this note to Lola. I'm asking her to meet me. A matter of great importance.

DU MESNIL: Who the hell is Lola?

CLOTILDE: Mrs. Simpson to you. We call her Lola—ever since she took that role in an operetta. She actually prefers the name. She thinks it suits her innerself.

DU MESNIL: Go on, write to "Lola." If she can succeed where a member of the French Academy has failed, I'll be delighted, but it will be a dark, dark day for France.

CLOTILDE: Leave France out of this. France doesn't worry about you, so don't you worry about France. *(Rising.)* Haven't you got something to do?

DU MESNIL: Yes, I intend to lock myself up in the wine cellar and drink myself to death.

CLOTILDE: I won't have it, Adolph. I won't have you making yourself sick over something as trivial as this.—Make yourself useful. Hand-carry this letter over to Mrs. Simpson. The fresh air will do you good. From there, you can go and see your uncle.

DU MESNIL: That old charlatan. I don't care if I ever set eyes on him again. I've had quite enough of his advice. He can find someone else to stick under his thumb.

CLOTILDE: Not at all. Everyone knows your uncle has been trying to get you this job, and if we do get it, it will be thanks to your uncle, period. You don't want people saying you owe this appointment to Mrs. Simpson or anyone in her circle. That wouldn't put you in a very good light.

DU MESNIL: You've got a point there. I'll drop this letter off and then get over to my uncle. The Treasury dinner party will just have to do without me.

CLOTILDE: Not at all! Why change your routine? You enjoy those stuffy dinners and big, black cigars. Lots of overweight gentlemen, patting their paunches and pretending they rule the roost. Why deprive yourself? You just carry on as usual, and I'll visit my old schoolmate who'd be very distressed not to see me.

DU MESNIL: But I'm still feeling a little low, Clotilde. I'd much rather stay with you.

CLOTILDE: Don't mope, Adolph. You can see me any time. Here!
(She gives him the letter and, as if he were a little boy, brushes his hair back and straightens his jacket. Still downhearted, he starts to exit.)

CLOTILDE: Throw your shoulders back, stick out your chin. Try to look a little cheerful. Never show your troubles to the outside world, Adolph. That'll only makes them worse.
(He trudges out. CLOTILDE puts on her hat and coat again. After a moment, DU MESNIL trudges back in.)

DU MESNIL: What do I *say* to uncle?

CLOTILDE: Whatever pops into your head.

DU MESNIL: I want it to be clearly understood that I'm going to this dinner under duress. I'm in a foul mood.

CLOTILDE: It will improve once you've had a little wine.

DU MESNIL: *(A new idea.)* Right. Drown one's sorrows. That's the best way to go. *(He trudges out.)*

CLOTILDE: It's like something out of "Madame Bovary." What would he do without me? I dread to think. It's always that way. Whenever there's two candidates for some plum position, one a modest little deserving fellow and the other some idiot with nothing to recommend him but his connections, the idiot will get it every time.—Fifty million Frenchmen seem to always get it wrong. If I'm lucky I may get out of this house before nightfall. *(She heads quickly to the door but as she opens it LAFONT is revealed in the doorway.)* Oh, no, no NO! —Tell me it's a mirage! *(Furiously, CLOTILDE turns from LAFONT and resolved not say a word, strides away.)*

LAFONT: You're angry because I'm back again. But here's the way it happened: I was on my way—honestly I was. I was going to put you out of my head till tomorrow—like we said. And then all of a sudden, I saw your husband coming home.—What could I do?—I was just about to greet him when I thought: "Oh dear, Clotilde probably doesn't want him to know I've been here, so I'd better lay low." So I ducked into a doorway and let him go past. He did come home, didn't he? I'm not hallucinating am I?

Then I'm afraid I slightly panicked. "I can't stay here," I said to myself. "Clotilde is waiting for Mrs. Simpson to arrive; you'll just be in the way; don't be an oaf." But it didn't look as if anyone was coming. "Her plan must've probably fallen through," I thought. "Perhaps in that case, Clotilde will be glad to see me." You can't condemn me for so harmless and tender a thought.

Then your husband came out. But that didn't really count. Then I looked again to see if Mrs. Simpson's cab was on the way. There was no sign of it, so I went up the front stairs. Oh I was trembling all over, in a really terrible state, and I would have just turned around and left if it hadn't been for one of those lucky coincidences *(Laughs nervously.)*—well it depends from whose standpoint one is looking at it whether it's lucky or not —but your husband had left the front door open and I thought to myself: That is Fate saying: Go up, go in, go to it.—So I did. It's all happened so inevitably, Clotilde; you can't be angry about a thing like that?

(CLOTILDE says nothing.)

LAFONT: Would you say something? *(Long beat.)* Just one word? *(Long beat.)* Nothing? *(Long beat.)* Well then, I suppose, we should just call it a day. I know you don't love me; I'm just in the way. I'm well aware of all that. But we can part good friends, can't we?

(Holds out his hand. CLOTILDE stays mum and motionless. LAFONT looks pathetically at his outstretched hand. Becomes more depressed and downbeat, slowly withdraws his hand then does an unexpected volte-face. Furiously.) Shall I tell you something? Yes, I think I will! You weren't expecting anyone! Mrs. Simpson or anyone else! You're going to see your lover. To dine with him. To make love to him. I'm not a fool you know. And I know exactly who it is. His name is Mercier—ERNEST MERCIER!

CLOTILDE:*(Turning then enunciating very clearly.)* Alfred Mercier.

LAFONT: *(After a beat.)* Al-fred...???

62 • HENRY BECQUE

CLOTILDE: Alfred Mercier.

LAFONT: *(Accusingly.)* Number 28 Madeleine Street!!!

CLOTILDE: *(Correcting him.)* Number 28 Madeleine Avenue.

LAFONT: *(Beat.)* Clotilde, are you joking or is this so? —It *is* the truth, isn't it? *(Weeping.)* Oh Clotilde, what have you done? You could have deceived me delicately—without blurting it all out. This is the end. This time, it is *really* the end! *(He starts moving out heavily, still weeping then suddenly stops, turns back.)* Is it the end, Clotilde? *(Clotilde says nothing.)* The end! *(He exits.)* *(CLOTILDE lets out an enormous sigh of relief, checks her watch and hurries off in the opposite direction. Blackout.)*

END OF ACT TWO

ACT THREE

The scene is the same. A few days later. The double door is now wide open. The center table has been arranged with a coffee-service. On the sofa, finishing his cup of coffee, sits SIMPSON, a handsome man in his early thirties. CLOTILDE is wearing a new and tasteful frock, obviously chosen to impress. She seems slightly ill at ease. ADELE is in attendance.

CLOTILDE: Now, Mr. Simpson, you're to do exactly as you would at your mother's house. No standing on ceremony.
SIMPSON: I see.
CLOTILDE: Take m'sieur's cup, Adele, and then you may go.
ADELE: You won't need me this afternoon, Madame?
CLOTILDE: No, Adele.
ADELE: As I told you, madame, my poor brother…
CLOTILDE: Yes, you told me, he's contracted bronchitis or neuralgia…
ADELE: Emphysemia actually, *(To SIMPSON.)* can barely draw a breath… *(Demonstrates.)*
CLOTILDE: *(Wanting rid of her.)* We can go into all that later, Adele.
ADELE: *(Sourly.)* As you wish, madame.
(She exits with the cups.)
CLOTILDE: *(Drawing closer to Simpson.)* It's really true then, you're actually leaving Paris.
SIMPSON: True, true.
CLOTILDE: And on this very day.
SIMPSON: I'm catching the seven o'clock express which should get me home at midnight.
CLOTILDE: Your trunks are all packed?
SIMPSON: My man is finishing them up as we speak.
CLOTILDE: And there's nothing I can do for you?
SIMPSON: There's very little time left and I wouldn't want to put you to any bother.
(CLOTILDE rises to place her cup on the table.)
CLOTILDE: And what does you mother think of this sudden departure?
SIMPSON: She's delighted to see me go. It's mainly on her account that I'm leaving so soon. She wants me to refurbish the house from top to bottom. When she moves into Croquingnole, she'd like it to be transformed.
CLOTILDE: If your mother approves, I suppose there is nothing more to say.

64 • HENRY BECQUE

SIMPSON: You're too much enamoured of Paris. For you it's never boring and you can't imagine living anywhere else.

CLOTILDE: It's not so much that. It's just that a man of your age and position wouldn't be leaving Paris if there was some…some strong attachment to keep him here. The winter is practically over; the weather has been miserable, it's true, yet no one thinks of leaving—except you. There must be some reason.

SIMPSON: I can think of more reasons for staying than going.

CLOTILDE: Then why go?

SIMPSON: I'm bored. Bored and irritated and a little humiliated. Sometimes I feel like a beggar in this city. Look at that dingy little ground-floor apartment of mine. I'm ashamed to live there and even more ashamed when anyone comes to visit. My mother refuses to set me up in the style to which *she* has become accustomed. She'd rather see me travel, and so I do, but get precious little satisfaction out of it.

It's different in the country, at Croquignole; there I'm a "somebody." The locals tip their hats to me as I pass by. I have everything I lack here—my horses, my dogs, my guns.—You know I've quite an impressive collection of blunderbusses—weapons dating back to the 17th century, and they all need to be cared for—just like pets. Cleaned and polished and hung just so.—Paris is a fine city; if I could live here with some self-respect, it might even be tolerable.

CLOTILDE: I feel this is my fault. I should have looked after you better. To think of separating now, after only four months…I hope it hasn't seemed too long.

SIMPSON: Five months.

CLOTILDE: Is it really?

SIMPSON: *(Counting on his fingers.)* January 15th, February 15th, March 15th…

CLOTILDE: You're right. Let's call it five months and let it go at that.

(There is a sticky pause in which CLOTILDE disguises the fact that she is quietly agonizing and SIMPSON feels he must in some way make amends.)

SIMPSON: *(Coming closer.)* You ought to come down to Croquignole. I'd love to show you my collection.

CLOTILDE: *(Smiling.)* Your blunderbuses.

SIMPSON: Perhaps in the summer, when my mother visits with some of her society friends.

CLOTILDE: Don't count on it. My husband can't get away very easily.

SIMPSON: He can always stay behind.

CLOTILDE: He doesn't much like being left behind.

SIMPSON: You'd find your friend Mrs. Beaulieu there. She doesn't seem to have any trouble travelling on her own.

CLOTILDE: I don't know very much about that. I'm close to Pauline; but we're not exactly bosom friends.

SIMPSON: It was she that introduced you to my mother.

CLOTILDE: But she never knew why I so much wanted that introduction—Are you insinuating that Mrs. Beaulieu is not as proper as she should be? Have you been listening to tittle-tattle again?

SIMPSON: I'm aware of one "grande folie"—with one of my friends.

CLOTILDE: And who is that?

SIMPSON: Hector de Godefroy.

CLOTILDE: You've been misinformed, my dear. For the past four years, Mrs. Beaulieu has been consorting with a charming young man who absolutely adores her and never leaves her side.

SIMPSON: And who is that?

CLOTILDE: *(After a moment's hesitation.)* Alfred Mercier.

SIMPSON: That may well be, but she's developed a grand passion for my friend Hector—I can't imagine why—and a day doesn't go by that she doesn't see him.

CLOTILDE: And where did you hear all that?

SIMPSON: From Mrs. Beaulieu herself. She gives me regular and graphic accounts of the entire affair.

CLOTILDE: What a child Pauline is. She can't lick a lollypop without describing the flavor to every passing stranger. I do wish she would exercise some restraint.

SIMPSON: That's another reason why I have to get out of here. One is knee-deep in scandal and it sucks you in like quicksand.

CLOTILDE: I hope you're not referring to my dear friend Pauline.

SIMPSON: She's in the quagmire as much as anyone else.

CLOTILDE: Pauline has suffered a great deal in her life.

SIMPSON: She seems to have come through with flying colors.

CLOTILDE: Perhaps you consoled her as well, from time to time.

SIMPSON: I never had the inclination.

CLOTILDE: Pauline is adorable.

SIMPSON: Still, I don't like to run with the herd.

CLOTILDE: Sometimes that's unavoidable.

SIMPSON: I don't think many of your lady-friends would acknowledge that.

CLOTILDE: And what does that prove? That we're weak, fickle, vulnerable people. That we're constantly being led astray; that we mingle with a lot of boorish men who don't know how to love us as we wish to be loved, or worse, ungrateful scoundrels who treat women merely as playthings.

You're probably right. The best course of action is to look at all men as if they were interchangeable. To shut our eyes, stop up our ears and say: "Here is your husband, your home. Just stick to it!" Life might be considerably less exciting, but we'd avoid all the turmoil, disillusionment and heartbreak. *(CLOTILDE is crying.)*

SIMPSON: What is it?

CLOTILDE: Leave me alone.

SIMPSON: Tears.

CLOTILDE: Real ones for a change.

SIMPSON: What are you crying about?

CLOTILDE: Who knows? There's a little bit of everything in a woman's tears.

SIMPSON: I'm sorry—if my leaving has…

CLOTILDE: *(Forcibly pulling herself together.)* No tremors of guilt please! They're totally uncalled for. It's the oldest story in the world. People come together; they like each other; they part. When men are first worming their way into our hearts, they're as tender and gentle as can be. But when they're tearing themselves away, they leave a sorry mess behind. I must call Adolph. —He'd leave us alone together till three in the morning, he's so trusting and gullible.

(Holding out her hand.) So let's say goodbye to one another. Think back fondly to these past five months—that's really all I ask. It was you that managed to get us what we wanted—and you provided that generous service after we'd become lovers. It wasn't really necessary, but it is appreciated. If one day, for some reason or other, you should travel back this way and pass by this house, please drop in. You know you will always be welcome.

SIMPSON: *(From the heart.)* You're very…charming.

CLOTILDE: I know it.—For all the good it does. *(Goes to the door.)* Adolph, do stop smoking now. And you can finish the paper later. Mr. Simpson is leaving and you must see him out.

(SIMPSON and CLOTILDE look at each other hard and long, feeling there is much more to be said, but that neither one can say it. After a moment, DU MESNIL enters.)

DU MESNIL: I'm an atrocious host, leaving you alone like this.

SIMPSON: It's quite all right.

DU MESNIL: I'm a creature of habit you know, and every day after lunch, I just pull out all the stops and drown myself in tobacco.

SIMPSON: Are you ready?

DU MESNIL: At your service.

SIMPSON: Let us go then.

(SIMPSON moves to the side and puts on his coat.)

DU MESNIL: *(Whispering to his wife.)* Should I be thanking this man in any special way?

CLOTILDE: No, we've had him to lunch. That's quite enough.

DU MESNIL: But we are greatly obliged to that friend of his in the government, shouldn't we…?

CLOTILDE: His mother attended to everything—after I wrote her, you remember.

DU MESNIL: I had no idea Mrs. Simpson had such a grown-up son. What do you make of him?

CLOTILDE: He's a gentleman.

DU MESNIL: What was he saying to you?

CLOTILDE: That I was perfect.

DU MESNIL: You mean as a hostess?

CLOTILDE: In every way.

DU MESNIL: That's an odd thing for him to say.

CLOTILDE: He's leaving Paris tonight.

DU MESNIL: Not coming back?

CLOTILDE: Not for a while.

SIMPSON: *(Returning to them.)* You'll excuse me for having to rush off like this. I seem to be missing Paris even before I've left it.

CLOTILDE: You'll forget it in time.

SIMPSON: Remember, you've a standing invitation for Croquignole. If I should have to get back to Paris for any reason—and if need be, I'll invent one—I'll try to persuade you again.

CLOTILDE: *(Giving her hand.)* Good-bye.

SIMPSON: *(Holding it too long.)* Good-bye. *(Then turning to DU MESNIL.)* M'sieur Du Mesnil.

DU MESNIL: Come along, I'll show you out. *(They leave.)*

(Left alone, CLOTILDE takes her coffee cup, moves to the bar and pours in a mixture of brandy, cognac and other strong liquors. Suddenly notices that SIMPSON has left his umbrella behind; instinctively picks it up as if to run after him—hesitates—takes hold of the handle as if it were the owner's hand—and then, deciding to keep it, secretes it in a closet. With her liquorized coffee cup, she wanders back to the sofa.)

CLOTILDE: A perfect gentleman—in every way. A little tiresome with his blunderbusses, perhaps. *(She sips from her coffee cup and shivers at the strength of the brew.)* It serves me right. I already had everything I ever needed. A home, a family, a husband, a dear friend, a second husband, as it were.—Oh, I abused him terribly. No one could blame him for slamming the door behind

him. He probably thought I was angrier than I actually was. Men understand so little. We're susceptible to those that charm us, even toy with us, but we always wind up with those that love us.
(The doorbell rings; CLOTILDE places the loaded coffee cup on the table. ADELE, in her coat and hat, ready to depart, enters in a flap.)
ADELE: It's M'sieur Lafont, madame!
CLOTILDE: Well, why are you so astonished announcing M'sieur Lafont?
ADELE: Shall I say you're out madame?
CLOTILDE: *Am* I out?
ADELE: Are you *in*?
CLOTILDE: Is your eyesight going, Adele? Along with everything else? Just run along. You wouldn't want to miss the last death-rattle of your rapidly departing brother.
(ADELE shows in LAFONT and exits hurriedly. LAFONT stands there for a moment, not quite sure how to deal with the situation. When he speaks it is in a very slow and measured manner, quite unnaturally.)
LAFONT: How—do—you—do.
CLOTILDE:*(In the same calculated manner.)* Quite—well—and—you.
LAFONT: Quite poorly. Miserably, in fact.—*(Back to his calculated voice.)* Do—I—disturb—you?
CLOTILDE: Not in the least.
LAFONT: You were on your way out perhaps?
CLOTILDE: I hardly go anywhere these days. Where *should* I go?
LAFONT: *(Taking in the coffee service.)* You had company for lunch?
CLOTILDE: Hardly company. Just one.
LAFONT: A friend?
CLOTILDE: An acquaintance.
LAFONT: Might—I—know—his—name?
CLOTILDE: My husband mentioned it, but it seems to have slipped my mind.
LAFONT: I saw them leave together.
CLOTILDE: Oh? So you were under my window with your eyes glued to the front door. If I'd known I'd have drawn the curtains and revealed myself to you.—*(Beat.)* It was very sweet of you—not to have forgotten me right away.
LAFONT:*(Cautiously.)* And who was that gentleman?
CLOTILDE: A mere acquaintance, as I said. He poses no threat to you. My husband introduced him to me this morning, and tonight, he departs Paris.
LAFONT: And all this is the truth?
CLOTILDE: Why should I lie to you now that I'm a torn-out leaf in your memory album. What would be the point?

You haven't changed very much; that's something in your favor. Come and sit in the easy chair and try not to pace back and forth or carry on as you did before. I have horrid memories of all that.

LAFONT: Clotilde.

CLOTILDE: There is no "Clotilde" any more. You dissolved her, remember?

LAFONT: *(Beginning to get het up.)* Clotilde!

CLOTILDE: Let's try to stay relaxed a little while longer.

LAFONT: I very much regret that ridiculous scene which could so easily have been prevented.—Alfred Mercier! *(CLOTILDE laughs.)* Well, what do you expect. I'd been eaten up by jealousy of this Mercier for a very long time. The thought of him kept me awake at night. Mrs. Beaulieu should be very grateful for your discretion.

CLOTILDE: Enough of all that. And what have you been doing since I saw you last?

LAFONT: Thinking of you.

CLOTILDE: That goes without saying. Anything else?

LAFONT: *(Nonchalantly.)* Life has gone on as usual—*(Miserably.)* bitterly, painfully, torturously.

CLOTILDE: Didn't you ever go on that trip you were planning?

LAFONT: I had the opportunity, but could not tear myself away from Paris.

CLOTILDE: Have the ladies been kind to you? Have you been well looked after?

LAFONT: I refuse to answer that.

CLOTILDE: But why? In the old days, I might have been wounded by your infidelities—even fatally so. But what was *verboten* then is perfectly permissible now. As if I didn't know you were the sort of man who couldn't possibly deny himself consolations.

LAFONT: I was much too inconsolable to think about any "consolations." And if Fate did take you from me forever, I would never dream of trying to replace you from those circles that I no longer frequent.

CLOTILDE: That's wrong. You should never abandon those ladies. They're the only completely free women in France. And they're not fragile. They love scenes and tears and squabbles and conflicts. You'll never get those things from me. All I can offer is a peaceful and sincere love, expecting nothing in return.

LAFONT: But that's exactly what I want. What we all want.

CLOTILDE: Then we must tread carefully, mustn't we? One wrong step and "whoosh."

LAFONT: *(Hungrily.)* Clotilde!

CLOTILDE: That has a certain familiar ring to it.

LAFONT: *(Pleadingly.)* Clotilde.

CLOTILDE: So has that.

LAFONT: Let me take your hand.

CLOTILDE: Certainly not.

LAFONT: Will you not give me your hand?

CLOTILDE: *(Beat.)* We'll see. *(LAFONT crumples.)* And don't give me *that* face or I'll throw you out at once.

LAFONT: Please, give me your hand!

(CLOTILDE makes a big scene of debating whether or not to yield her hand to LAFONT and, after a prolonged deliberation, extends it. LAFONT grasps it at once and kisses it.)

CLOTILDE: Now I suppose you'll want the other one as well.

(She extends it. LAFONT kisses it as well, then realizing there is something amiss, drops both.)

LAFONT: You are distant, remote.

CLOTILDE: I allowed you to sit beside me. I gave you my hand. Both of them in fact. Did you expect me to throw off my clothes and prostrate myself the moment you came in?

LAFONT: I am scoundrel. I admit it. You may pile reproaches on to my head until I sink into the ground.—But you deserve some as well.

CLOTILDE: No thank you.

LAFONT: *(Getting hot under the collar.)* Whose fault was it that our relations suddenly changed? Mine or yours? There was no happier man on the face of the earth—until you turned everything upside down.

CLOTILDE: I? Only you could have done that—would have done it—if I hadn't stopped you.

LAFONT: *(About to leap into the fray, suddenly changes course.)* You're right. I'm sorry I brought it up.—Water under the bridge.

CLOTILDE: Black, muddy, filthy water it is too. I allow you in. I listen to your explanations; begin to feel you genuinely regret your atrocious behavior, persuade myself that if you were truly to reform, I might just see my way clear to forgiving you—and then that old devil in you reappears, brandishing his pitchfork and kicking with his cloven hoofs.—No, Lafont, there is no water-*under*-the-bridge, it's all above the bridge—being poured over my head. —Get away.

LAFONT: But why?

CLOTILDE: I want to get up.

LAFONT: Please.

CLOTILDE: No!

LAFONT: Let's stay as we are.

CLOTILDE: Let's not.
LAFONT: Have I upset you?
CLOTILDE: I'm nervous and agitated…
LAFONT: All the more reason…
CLOTILDE: For what?
LAFONT: That you sit down.
CLOTILDE: Such logic!
LAFONT: *I'm* agitated as well!
CLOTILDE: Then you should take a long, cold shower, shouldn't you?
>   *(They both subside. CLOTILDE takes out a cigarette. LAFONT is immediately there with his cigarette lighter. It doesn't work. He tries again. It still doesn't ignite. He goes for a match; strikes it then accidentally blows it out. He strikes another. It burns his finger. Flicking it away, he accidentally knocks the cigarette out of CLOTILDE'S mouth. To make amends, he offers her one from his pack. She stares coldly at the pack—causing him to examine it. He tips it upside down. It is empty. CLOTILDE sighs, indicating that she no longer wants to smoke. LAFONT, more nervous than ever, takes up CLOTILDE'S coffee cup and takes a swig of what he believes to be coffee. Of course, it is the remains of CLOTILDE'S diabolically mixed drink. He gags on it, clears his throat and regains controls of himself.)*

LAFONT: You were thinking of forgiving me, you said.
CLOTILDE: I'm afraid that was a rather hasty thought.
LAFONT: Why can't we just pick up where we left off?
CLOTILDE: You'll never be happy with me, Lafont. And you'll never understand my situation.
LAFONT: What situation?
CLOTILDE: Am I or am I not a married woman? Am I or am I not entirely dependent on my husband who is entitled to find me in our home whenever he wishes. That's the least a wife can do, wouldn't you say?—Then there's another problem.
LAFONT: Another problem?
CLOTILDE: You don't like my husband.
LAFONT: But I do; I really do!
CLOTILDE: No you don't; not really. Your temperments are very different.
LAFONT: But that's just not so. Your husband never had but two friends in the whole world.
CLOTILDE: Two?
LAFONT: Yes, two.
CLOTILDE: Who?
LAFONT: Why you and me.

(CLOTILDE, *about to protest, is silenced for a moment. Considers the idea then bursts out laughing. LAFONT, happy to share a laugh with her, joins in uncomprehendingly.*)

LAFONT: Let's just talk about ourselves for a moment. You know, don't you, that I am mad about you.

CLOTILDE: I think I suit your taste, if that's what you mean.

LAFONT: And I suit yours as well. —You don't come across a love like mine every day. Do you?

CLOTILDE: It's because I know very well that you feel so deeply that I've put up with all your…lunacies.

LAFONT: In normal circumstances, I am very tender, very caring, very affectionate…

CLOTILDE: You can certainly be very pleasant when you want to be. You sometimes have a very agreeable way of putting things. And you don't go on about blunderbusses.

LAFONT: Ey?

CLOTILDE: Never mind.

LAFONT:*(Drawing nearer.)* Then tell me you forgive me.

CLOTILDE:*(Weakening.)* Oh, Lafont.

LAFONT: You do forgive me, don't you?

CLOTILDE:*(Weakening.)* Yes. Now be a good boy.

LAFONT: You forgive me, everything.

CLOTILDE: I've said I do. What more do you want?

(LAFONT *is now so close, he is almost crawling on top of her. Remembering where she is,* CLOTILDE *draws away.*)

CLOTILDE: Now don't get too lively.—I'll come to see you.

LAFONT: When?

CLOTILDE: Whenever it's convenient.

LAFONT: *(Amorously.)* Clo-tilde.

CLOTILDE:*(She examines him.)* You love me?

LAFONT: I adore you.

(LAFONT, *thinking he is back at the sacred fount again, moves towards her.* CLOTILDE *rises suddenly, leaving him high and dry.*)

CLOTILDE: What a very long, winding journey to get back to exactly where we were.

LAFONT: Do you regret it?

CLOTILDE: Not yet.

LAFONT: I was almost suicidal when I got here. I shall leave in a much more tranquil state.

CLOTILDE: Well I hope you've learned your lesson. And no more tantrums, do you hear? If you ever feel one coming on again, let's just sit down and talk things over quietly.—Do you promise?

LAFONT: I promise, my darling.

CLOTILDE: Now listen; I've something to tell you that I think will please you. *(LAFONT lights up.)* My friendship with Mrs. Simpson is entirely over.

LAFONT: You've quarreled with her?

CLOTILDE: On the contrary; she's done me a very great favor for which I will always be grateful. It's not so much Mrs. Simpson herself—as her house that I intend to avoid.

LAFONT: I told you that was a disreputable place. I told you so.

CLOTILDE: Well, you're obviously much shrewder than I in such matters.

LAFONT: And there's someone else you should break with as well.

CLOTILDE: Oh, and who's that?

LAFONT: Mrs. Beaulieu.

CLOTILDE: What, break with Pauline? Whatever for?

LAFONT: It seems to me…

CLOTILDE: It seems to you—what?

LAFONT: Alfred Mercier—that's what. I know very well what's going on between those two. In fact, everyone in Paris knows.

CLOTILDE: What of it?

LAFONT: *(Shocked.)* You can't possibly condone such behavior!

CLOTILDE: Are you going to blame Pauline for doing for Mercier exactly what I'm doing for you?

LAFONT: It's not the same thing at all.

CLOTILDE: What's the difference?

LAFONT: There is one, I assure you.

CLOTILDE: But you can't describe it.

LAFONT: No, but it's definitely there.

CLOTILDE: Oh, you men! It's all right for the goose, but not for the gander.—Instead of going on about Pauline, you should be thinking about my husband. He's constantly complaining that you never come round any more. He wants to know why.

(There is a sound of a door shutting.)

LAFONT: *(Pointing to the door.)* Was that Adolph that just came in?

CLOTILDE: Of course, it's Adolph. He does live here, remember. Better come up with a good story.

(LAFONT feels trapped for a moment and DU MESNIL enters.)

DU MESNIL: Lafont, is it you!

LAFONT: *(Embarrassed.)* Hello Adolph.

DU MESNIL: Why it's been weeks since we've—

LAFONT: *(Nervously.)* How are you, old chap?

DU MESNIL: Fine, but you haven't answered my question. Why did you drop out of sight like that. Where have you been? That's no way to treat old friends.

CLOTILDE: Don't badger him, Adolph. He's had a big problem.

DU MESNIL: A problem? What kind of problem?

CLOTILDE:*(To LAFONT.)* Shall *I* tell him?

LAFONT: If you like.

DU MESNIL: Come on, out with it, out with it.

CLOTILDE: He's been sick with jealousy.

DU MESNIL: Jealousy? *(To LAFONT.)* What! At your age?—I don't believe it. Who the devil are you jealous of? Some woman, I suppose. Some woman who belongs to someone else. It really takes the cake. These gay bachelors, they can't deny themselves anything. And then, they're jealous into the bargain. You know a famous economist came up with a definition of jealousy. Jealousy, he said, is nothing more nor less than being deprived of something one wants. Now if you were married, Lafont, you wouldn't be deprived—ipso facto—you wouldn't be jealous. *(To CLOTILDE.)* Am I right or not?

CLOTILDE: That's enough, Adolph.

DU MESNIL: Jealous! What a lame excuse. —*(He pours two cups of coffee.)* Oh, Clotilde have you told him?

CLOTILDE: What?

DU MESNIL: About the appointment.

CLOTILDE: Lafont was the first to write and congratulate you, don't you remember?

DU MESNIL: That's right. I forgot. He wrote instead of coming over. *(To LAFONT but looking at CLOTILDE to whom he hands one of the cups of coffee.)* It was my uncle you know, old Jean-Baptiste, who pulled it off for me.

CLOTILDE: Everyone knows it was your uncle, Adolph. It doesn't have to be shouted from the rooftops.

DU MESNIL: Well, it's better to have an office in the Treasury than to be jealous, ey Lafont. Oh, he's still in a bit of sulk about it all. His nose is still a little out of joint, I see.—Was she spreading it around town, is that it? Playing the field, and all that?

(LAFONT squirms visibly. CLOTILDE enjoys his discomfort.)

CLOTILDE: Adolph is asking you a question. Why don't you answer him.

LAFONT: What can I say. *(He absentmindedly picks up the liquor-filled coffee cup.)* Is there a man in Paris, or all the world for that matter, who can swear his mistress has never deceived him. Mine swears she hasn't. She's not very likely to say she had. But the main thing is: We've made it up—and I think that's the best solution for all concerned.

CLOTILDE: It's a good thing the lady in question isn't around to hear the opinion you have of her—or she might box your ears.— But when you stop to consider it, in the long run, it's fidelity that makes the world go round, don't you think?

(LAFONT and CLOTILDE turn to DU MESNIL.)

DU MESNIL: *(Piously.)* I've always believed that, my dear. Always.

(He takes a drink from his coffee-cup; so does CLOTILDE; and so does LAFONT whose cup, unfortunately, is still loaded with the mixture of deadly liquors. A "take" and the curtain falls.)

END OF PLAY

QUACK

A Musical Version of Molière's
The Physician In Spite of Himself

Freely Adapted and with Lyrics
by Charles Marowitz
Music by Michael Valenti

Quack was first presented by the Cal Rep Theatre Company in Long Beach, California on November 2, 1996 with the following cast.

MARTI	Susan Watson
ORVILLE	Matt Gourley
BIG ROB	Michael Pando
VALMOTH	John Shepard
LUCIEN	Davis Mejia
GERALDO	Peter Zapp
LUCY-LYNN	Katie Johnson
EVANGELINE	Deanna Boyd
LEOPOLD	Matthew Gitkin

Music Director: Michael Valenti
Choreography: Holly Harbinger
Accompanist: Ron Woyshner
Director: Charles Marowitz

CAST OF CHARACTERS
MARTI, Orville's wife
ORVILLE, a Lumberjack
BIG ROB, his Neighbor,
VALMOTH, a Country Gent,
LUCIEN, his friend
GERALDO, a Country Squire
LUCY-LYNN, his Daughter
EVANGELINE, a Governess
LEOPOLD, in love with Lucy-Lynn
TWO MAIDS

SETTING
Quack takes place on a vaudeville stage. Large old-fashioned proscenium arch embossed with cherubs; a serious bust of Molière on one side; a serious bust of Groucho Marx on the other. A runway with racer-lighting runs from the center of the stage out into the auditorium. All props and costumes have the crude simplicity they would have in a vaudeville show. The musicians, wearing striped shirts with garters on their arms, bowler hats and moustaches, are visible Auditorium Left. On the Right of the stage, an easel with "enunciators" announces the title of each musical number.

SCENE ONE

Backcloth of the Great Outdoors. A few objects strewn around. A tire; a saw; an ax; a paddle; an oil can, a pair of slapsticks; two tree stumps. Enunciator sign on easel at side reads: MARTI and ORVILLE: FIGHT SONG.

To the accompaniment of nervy, excitable music, MARTI stomps out; an angry ORVILLE is hard on her heels.

ORVILLE: I say I will!
MARTI: I say you won't!
ORVILLE: I say I do!
MARTI: I say you don't!
ORVILLE: Don't contradict!
MARTI: Don't raise your voice.
ORVILLE: D'y' wanna get kicked?
MARTI: Do I have a choice?
ORVILLE: I'm the one who wears the pants in this here family.
MARTI: With flys unbuttoned everywhere for all the world to see!?
ORVILLE: It's just the way I say it is!
MARTI: What a grouchy geezer.
ORVILLE: I'm getting into such a tiz!
MARTI: You're gonna have a seizure.
ORVILLE: I don't want a wife with whom I always have to fight.
MARTI: A woman's husband needs to knows his wife is always right.
BOTH: O marital bliss—a cuddle and kiss
A clang of the wedding bell.
ORVILLE: A honyemoon often
MARTI: Winds up in a coffin
BOTH: And Heaven just turns into hell.

(Dialogue—vamp under.)

ORVILLE: Don't argue! If I say no, I mean No.
MARTI: And if you say yes?
ORVILLE: I still mean No.
MARTI: I didn't get married to have a chain put around my neck.

QUACK • 79

ORVILLE:	No, you'd rather put a noose around mine! — I must've been drunk when I proposed to you.
MARTI:	Why would that day've been different from any other?
ORVILLE:	I say I'm right!
MARTI:	I say you're not!
ORVILLE:	You're none too bright!
MARTI:	And you're a clot!
ORVILLE:	Have some respect!
MARTI:	For you? —Tut tut.
ORVILLE:	Be cirumspect!
MARTI:	Go kiss my butt!
ORVILLE:	You said that you would marry me for better or for worse.
MARTI:	But nothing's getting better and what's worse is getting worse.
BOTH:	O marital bliss—a cuddle and kiss A clang of the wedding bell.
ORVILLE:	A honyemoon often
MARTI:	Winds up in a coffin
BOTH:	And Heaven just turns into hell.

(Dialogue—vamp under.)

ORVILLE:	Don't interrupt when I'm talking.
MARTI:	Don't talk when I'm interrrupting!
ORVILLE:	A wife should be obedi-ent.
MARTI:	(Boy, this guy is tacky.)
ORVILLE:	That is what the preacher meant.
MARTI:	You just want a lackey.
ORVILLE:	A husband's like a Judge who hammers law in with his spikes
MARTI:	A wife is like a higher court repealing what she likes.
BOTH:	O marital bliss—a cuddle and kiss A clang of the wedding bell.
ORVILLE:	A honyemoon often
MARTI:	Winds up in a coffin
BOTH:	And Heaven just turns into hell.

ORVILLE: Aristotle was so right when he said: there's no devil in hell worse than a she-devil of a wife.

MARTI: You heard him, did you?

ORVILLE: Heard who?

MARTI: Your Aristotle.

ORVILLE: How could I have heard him—that was years ago.

MARTI: So it's just hearsay.

ORVILLE: You're really getting my goat!

MARTI: Always showing off your great knowledge. You who were kicked out of the fifth grade.

ORVILLE: *(Defensively.)* I wasn't kicked out, I told you, I was transferred.

MARTI: Transferred back to the second!

ORVILLE: You just can't stand the fact that when I worked as a hospital orderly for six years I picked up a whole medical education. There isn't another woodchopper in the whole country who can say that.

MARTI: Must come in pretty handy—chopping trees.

ORVILLE: While I was developing my mind, you were out peddling your ass.

MARTI: And don't think there weren't takers!!! You'd been a bachelor so long, you thought making love took place in two separate beds.

ORVILLE: Don't start on that…

MARTI: You'd never even seen a condom before. You thought it was a shower cap for your pecker.

ORVILLE: I'm warning you…

MARTI: If I hadn't drawn you a diagram, you'd have stuck it in the wall plug!

ORVILLE: Enough, I say! You were damn lucky I came along.

MARTI: And look at me now. All my clothes come from the Thrift Store, you work only three days out of every month and you've hocked almost every piece of furniture we own.

ORVILLE: It'll make moving a lot easier.

MARTI: Last week you even hocked the bath tub.

ORVILLE: *You* never used it!

MARTI: You spend all day drinking, smoking or gambling. And what am I supposed to do with the family? I've got four mouths to feed.

ORVILLE: *(Aside.)* And I've got one big one to listen to.

MARTINE: How much longer do you think I'm going to take this?

ORVILLE: Calm down.

MARTI: There's gonna be some changes around here, let me tell you.

ORVILLE: You're asking for it, Marti.

MARTI: This is the Age of the Woman, haven't you heard?

ORVILLE: It's The Age of the Aging Woman, as far as you're concerned.

MARTI: You don't faze me, y'know.

ORVILLE: I'm warning you.

MARTI: Guzzler.

ORVILLE: Don't push it.

MARTI: Jackass!

ORVILLE: You're asking for it.

MARTI: Pisspot!

ORVILLE: Marti—

MARTI: Peabrain! Pig-Mouth! Snorkle-Nose! —Dickhead!

ORVILLE: *(Erupting.)* That's it; that's it!

> *(ORVILLE grabs the nearby paddle and begins paddling MARTI's bottom. She tries to escape but he intercepts her on all sides and keeps paddling. When the beating reaches its height, BIG ROB, a lumberjack, enters and snatches the paddle out of ORVILLE's hands.)*

BIG ROB: Hey that's a bit heavy—whackin' your wife.

MARTI: *(Beat—then confronting him directly.)* What business is it of yours?

BIG ROB: Huh?

MARTI: Suppose I want to be whacked.

BIG ROB: Want to be…?

MARTI: Who asked you to put your oar in?

> *(Both do a "take" on paddle as MARTI grabs it out of his hands.)*

BIG ROB: If you enjoy that kind'a thing…

MARTI: And what if I do?

BIG ROB: Well it's entirely up to you.

MARTI: You're goddam right it is! *(To ORVILLE.)* Look at this mug interfering with a happily married couple.

MARTI: Is it any of *your* business?

BIG ROB: None at all.

MARTI: Who asked you to butt in?

BIG ROB: Nobody.

MARTI: Maybe I like to be whacked around.

BIG ROB: Chacun à son gout.

MARTI: *(Thinking she's been insulted, threateningly.)* What did you say?!

BIG ROB: *(Defensively.)* To each his own.

MARTI: *(Threateningly.)* His own what?

BIG ROB: Whatever, whatever.

MARTI: If there's one thing that really gets my blood boiling, it's a goddam busybody. *(She bangs the paddle down on BIG ROB's foot. He hops backwards colliding with ORVILLE.)*

BIG ROB: *(Confidentially, to ORVILLE.)* Sorry I interfered. You can beat the hell out of her. I'll even give you a hand if you like.

ORVILLE: But I *don't* like.

BIG ROB: Then forget about it.

ORVILLE: If I want to whack her, I'll whack her and if I don't want to whack her, I won't whack her,

BIG ROB: *(Backing down.)* That seems reasonable.

ORVILLE: She's my wife, isn't she?

BIG ROB: Yeah, *(Under.)* thank God.

ORVILLE: What?

BIG ROB: You do just as you like!

ORVILLE: Damn right I will.

BIG ROB: Would you like me to get you the paddle? *(He hurries it over to ORVILLE.)*

ORVILLE: Are you trying to teach me how to whack my own wife?

BIG ROB: Never entered my mind.

ORVILLE: Remember what Cicero said: Never stick your fingers in a hornet's nest or your nose into your neighbor's washing.
(As BIG ROB turns to check out MARTI, ORVILLE whacks him with the paddle and BIG ROB hobbles out.)

BIG ROB: *(Offstage—taking revenge.)* He also said: People who carry big sticks always have small peckers!
(ORVILLE simmers down, turns to MARTI who is still scowling at him. He looses a slow, gradual smile in her direction. She subsides and returns the smile. Having played out their sado-masochistic game to their own satisfaction, they fall into each other's arms. But MARTI's bottom still smarts and she suddenly pulls out of the embrace as angry as before.)

MARTI: What do you mean whacking me like that?

ORVILLE: A love pat.

MARTI: The hell it was.

ORVILLE: A sign of affection.

MARTI: It hurts.

ORVILLE: Shall I kiss it better?

MARTI: It stings; it's bruised.

ORVILLE: Nobody's gonna see it.

MARTI: What makes you think not?

ORVILLE: *(A take for both.)* Let's kiss and make up.

MARTI: You think you can always kiss and make up.

ORVILLE: Don't be mad. You enjoyed it.

MARTI: My backside's black and blue. *(Rubbing it.)* It hurts.

ORVILLE: Don't be a pain in the ass.

(MARTI and ORVILLE share a take.)

ORVILLE: A little kiss and make up.

(ORVILLE opens his arms. MARTI studies him for a moment then deliberately decides to bury the hatchet. She enters the embrace but then in an aside to us…)

MARTI: *(Aside.)* This is one he's gonna pay for. A battered wife, like an elephant, never forgets.

ORVILLE: It's silly to get uptight, Marti. A marriage without a few good whacks in it is like a day without sunshine.

MARTI: Who said that?

ORVILLE: I did—are you going deaf? Now I'm off to chop some wood. I'm working on a big order for a company up north. Lots of moolah soon. What would you like me to get you?

MARTI: A mustard plaster and a hot compress.

(ORVILLE smiles at his wife's wit, puckers his lips into a few audible kisses and leaves.)

MARTI: I'm getting sick and tired of his horny little games. *(Rubbing her posterior.)* This time he's gone too far. I'm gonna hatch me a revenge that he won't soon forget. *(Takes a small effigy of ORVILLE out of her dress and studiously begins sticking pins into it.)*

(VALMOTH and LUCIAN, dressed in knickerbockers and tweeds, enter. LUCIAN holds a rifle. VALMOTH, a shooting stick. Both men appear to be upper-class and out for a little grouse shoot.)

LUCIEN: It's a real worry, Valmoth. Who knows how it'll turn out.

VALMOTH: We have to do what the old man says. Y'know he's as stubborn as they come. If the girl can recover, the marriage will go through and Horatio will cart her away. Although she seems to prefer this Leopold-fellow but the old man will never accept him into the family.

LUCIEN: What's he going to come up with next. None of those doctors seem to know what they're doing.

VALMOTH: He's checked out every alternative medicine he can lay his hands on. He's already tried faith healing, acupuncture, mineral baths, macrobiotics and colonic irrigation. Who knows what'll come next.

(MARTI, who has been cogitating her revenge, hasn't seen the strangers enter. She absentmindedly bumps into them.)

MARTI: Oh sorry. I was working out something in my head and I didn't see you.

VALMOTH: We've all got problems we're trying to work out, madame.

MARTI: Oh. Is there something I might be able to help you with?

VALMOTH: I doubt it. Some of the best minds in the country have tried to solve our problems—all to no avail.

MARTI: Sounds serious.

VALMOTH: Just imagine this, madame. A young and beautiful girl who has everything to live for, suddenly struck with a rare disease that robs her of her powers of speech. Her father summons doctors from every corner of the globe—but no one can find the answer. He's tried every remedy known to medical science, and now he's trying all the others.—If only some truly gifted specialist could be found to get to the bottom of it all—that would seem to be the only hope.

MARTI: *(Aside.)* Something's cooking in the old noggin. Something tasty, like a sweet revenge.—This is a fateful meeting, gentlemen—although I don't usually believe in fate. There's a fellow here, a very special kind of specialist, who's had miraculous results all over the world. Everybody's after him. Kings, princes, sheiks, emperors. That's why he's come to this remote part of the world to get away from all those bothersome offers.

LUCIEN: Really, where could we find this man?

MARTI: He's out there—chopping wood.

LUCIEN: A doctor? Chopping wood.

MARTI: That's the whole point, y'see: to be incognito. If you saw him now, you'd think this is just an ordinary lumberjack—which is exactly what he'd like you to think. He keeps all his genius well locked away and he's sworn never to practice medicine again.

VALMOTH: *(To LUCIEN.)* I've met this type before. Great healers with immense gifts who are a little eccentric.

MARTI: Eccentric, that's just the word for it. In order for him to admit he has these powers, you sometimes have to beat it out of him. That's what we had to do when we needed him to cure some local patients. We actually had to beat the truth out of him.

LUCIEN: And did he then confess it?

MARTI: Yes, but only then.

LUCIEN: A strange abberation.

MARTI: Ey?

LUCIEN: I say a strange abberation.

MARTI: Oh he's performed some very "strange abberations"—all over the country. But not until they beat it out of him.

VALMOTH: What name does he go under?

MARTI: His real name is—well I better not tell you that. But he goes under the name of Orville. That's the only name he'll answer to.

VALMOTH: "Orville." What a strange affectation.

MARTI: Ey?

VALMOTH: I say, a strange affectation.

MARTI: Oh he's done lots of those—some with anaesthetic and some without.

VALMOTH: Amazing.

LUCIEN: But is he really so gifted?

MARTI: He's a regular miracle worker. Six months ago there was a woman who lived up in the hills, she'd been given up by all the other doctors. A hopeless case, they said. They gave her the last rites and were getting ready to lay her out. Then, at the last minute, they decided to bring in this very special specialist…

VALMOTH: This Orville?

MARTI: Right. He refused of course; said he knew nothing about it; wouldn't even come. They gave him a few kicks and punches and finally got him over to her sick bed. He gave her a pinch of something or other—nobody quite knew what it was—and in an hour, the old lady was dancing around the room.

LUCIEN: Dancing you say?

MARTI: They couldn't stop her. She danced all the way into town and before she was through, she'd won first prize at the Harvest Moon ball.

VALMOTH: And she'd been given up for dead?

MARTI: They had the casket all made up. Clumps of flowers stacked by the graveside.

VALMOTH: Amazing reincarnation.

MARTI: Ey?

VALMOTH: I say, amazing reincarnation.

MARTI: Carnations, petunias, the whole works. —And just three weeks ago, a twelve-year-old boy stumbled off the belfry, landed on the paving stone and fractured his arms and legs, and split his head in six different places. Well they strong-armed this special specialist…

LUCIEN: Orville?

MARTI: Right. He rubbed the boy with some precious fluids which only he knew how to mix, and in the blink of an eye, the patient leapt up, jumped onto a bicycle and pedaled off to play shortstop with his Little League team. They won—twelve to two.

VALMOTH: The man must be touched with genius.

MARTI: Oh he's touched all right.

LUCIEN: Look, that must be him. The lumberjack.

MARTI: That's him. Remember now, it won't be easy. He'll never admit to it.

LUCIEN: If all it takes is a few punches, we'll bring him round all right, never fear.

MARTI: Yeah, the harder the punches, the better treatment he'll give. That's always the way.

VALMOTH: This has been a truly providential meeting, madame. And I thank you for this valuable information.

(MARTI, unseen by the two men, makes a "fongoo" gesture in ORVILLE'S direction, rubs her sore ass and Exits. ORVILLE, carrying a mountain-styled jug, enters, his axe at his belt. He's been at the jug and is in a tipsily happy state. As he approaches, VALMOTH and LUCIEN make themselves scarce. ORVILLE is singing to his jug.)

ORVILLE:
    Oh glug, glug, glug
    My little brown jug,
    You set me all agog.
    I take a slug
    Gluggedy-glug-glug
    And down goes all the grog.

    Everybody fancies you
    And wants a little sip.
    But you're true
    Like I am to you
    So come to my loving lip.

CHORUS:
    Booze, booze boo'soms are bonnie
    And yet, and yet and yet…
    There's nothing more scrumptious
    To make you feel bumptious
    As a touch of, not much of, the Glorious Wet.

    So glug, glug, glug.
    My little brown jug
    So round and full and nice.
    A little fire
    Slakes my desire
    And the rest is Paradise.

Bacchus knew you way back when
The grapes grew on the vine.
And many men
Have had you since then
But now you're mine, all mine.

CHORUS:
Booze, booze boo'soms are bonnie
And yet, and yet and yet...
There's nothing more scrumptious
To make you feel bumptious
As a touch of, not, much of, the Glorious Wet.

(As he drinks, VALMOTH and LUCIEN appear, each with a flask in hand. To ingratiate themselves with ORVILLE, they toast him with their flasks and all join in the chorus.)

ALL:
Booze, booze boo'soms are bonnie
And yet, and yet and yet...
There's nothing more scrumptious
To make you feel bumptious
As a touch of, not much of, the Glorious Wet.

(As the song ends, ORVILLE suddenly realizes he's been carousing with strangers, becomes suspicious and draws his jug close to his bosom.)

VALMOTH: Beg pardon, but is your name Orville?
ORVILLE: *(Suspciously.)* Depends.
VALMOTH: Depends? On what?
ORVILLE: On who wants to know.
VALMOTH: We simply want to convey our warmest greetings.
ORVILLE: Oh, in that case, it is. *(Ssuddenly withdraws his hand.)* Warmest greetings for what?
VALMOTH: We're delighted to make your acquaintance. We've been, as it were...
LUCIEN: Referred. We've been referred to you by a...a...
VALMOTH: A close friend who thought you might be able to...to
LUCIEN: Lend a hand...a helping-hand, as it were...to provide some...
VALMOTH: Services. Yes, some services.

ORVILLE: If it's got to do with business gentlemen, I am entirely at your service.

VALMOTH: We've been told of your excellent qualities.

ORVILLE: Best goddam timber for a thousand miles around. Kindling wood—raw lumber—tent poles—you name it.

VALMOTH: But...

ORVILLE: And you'll find the price reasonable. I've got testimonials from hundreds of satisfied customers. Firewood fifty dollars a cord—discount on quantity, of course.

VALMOTH: We needn't get into that right now.

ORVILLE: It can't go for any less. That's the going rate.

LUCIEN: We've been told....

ORVILLE: If you've been told then you know that's the going rate.

VALMOTH: Please don't be silly, Mr. Orville.

ORVILLE: Nothing silly about it. I'm not about to come down on the price. I've got a wife and four kids to support.

VALMOTH: Let's approach this from another standpoint....

ORVILLE: You can try other mills. You might get it cheaper. But what kind of wood will it be? Bent twigs and scrawny branches, maybe. But not quality wood. I cut the best. Everyody around here knows that.

VALMOTH: Can we change the subject.

ORVILLE: I've got overheads y'know.

LUCIEN: This is so irritating.

ORVILLE: I don't bilk my customers. What you see is what you get and what you get is the best I got.

VALMOTH: Why do you feel it necessary to go on in this vein, sir. It's an insult to us and an insult to yourself. A sage doctor, a peerless physician and healer trying to pass himself off as a lowly woodman; to withold his talents from a world that is crying out for them. —What a sordid spectacle.

ORVILLE: *(Beat: then confidentially to LUCIEN.)* Is he quite all right? I mean... *(Tapping his head.)*

LUCIEN: *(Slyly, inching over to him.)* It's all right you know, we know.

ORVILLE: Know? *(Looks to VALMOTH.)*

VALMOTH: *(Nods and taps his finger to his nose knowingly.)*
(ORVILLE looks again to LUCIEN who winks and nods. Then back to VALMOTH who smiles knowingly, taps his forehead and clucks. Instinctively, ORVILLE feels for the axe at his belt, as if to protect himself from deranged people.)

VALMOTH: No need to dissemble with us, old man.

ORVILLE: No?
VALMOTH: Not at all. We'll keep your secret.
ORVILLE: You will?
LUCIEN: If that's what you want.
ORVILLE: Uh huh.
VALMOTH: No one need know—except we three.
ORVILLE: The three of us.
VALMOTH: So long as you agree to come along.
ORVILLE: Come along?
VALMOTH: You know, and do your stuff.
ORVILLE: My stuff?—
LUCIEN: Give us some of your precious fluids.
   (ORVILLE instinctively protects his crotch.)
VALMOTH: We know you've done your stuff with sheiks and princes and emperors.
ORVILLE: What the hell're you talking about!!??
VALMOTH: We know very well you're a remarkable physician.
LUCIEN: And it's to your credit.
ORVILLE: Physician?
VALMOTH: Healer, specialist, whatever you want to call it.
ORVILLE: *(Beat.)* Gentlemen, I'm afraid we're all laboring under a delusion here. I'm no physician.
   (LUCIEN and VALMOTH look knowingly at each other; decide to humor the eccentric.)
VALMOTH: Of course you're not.
LUCIEN: A physician, chopping wood?
VALMOTH: Like an ordinary lumberjack?
   (Both LUCIEN and VALMOTH burst into forced laughter.)
VALMOTH: *(Suddenly earnest.)* Now just come along with us. We've got a very pressing case for you you to examine. We'll make it worth your while.
ORVILLE: Take your goddam hands off of me!
VALMOTH: Don't force us to take extreme measures.
LUCIEN: We simply wish to get a hold of your medical expertise.
ORVILLE: *(Protecting his crotch.)* You do and I'll chop off your fingers!
VALMOTH: We've heard all about your accomplishments.
ORVILLE: I don't know what you're talking about?
LUCIEN: *(To VALMOTH.)* It's no use, we'll have to do what she said.
VALMOTH: I implore you—one last time.
LUCIEN: Admit you're a doctor. *(As to a child.)* Just 'fess it right up.

VALMOTH: What's the point in denying it?

ORVILLE: I'm telling you calmly and reasonably. You've got the wrong man. I'm no doctor.

VALMOTH: Are you telling us that you're not a physician.

ORVILLE: I'm not a physician!

LUCIEN: Not a healer—not a specialist?

ORVILLE: I'm not a healer! —Not a specialist!

(*VALMOTH gives a signal to LUCIEN. VALMOTH and LUCIEN, using paddles, begin whalloping ORVILLE around the stage. He tries to escape but they are relentless. Finally they get him down on his stomach and paddle the be-Jesus out of him.*)

ORVILLE: All right. I'm a doctor! I'm a healer! I'm a specialist. I'm anything you like. Only knock it off!

VALMOTH: (*Tuckered out.*) Why do you force civilized people to indulge in these violent antics. It's really too much.

LUCIEN: (*Breathing heavy.*) I'm quite winded.

ORVILLE: How do you think I feel? —Is this some kind of joke? Gentlemen, you know very well I'm no doctor.

VALMOTH: Are you reneging?

LUCIEN: Still insisting you're not a doctor?

ORVILLE: Do I look like a doctor? Come on now.

(*LUCIEN looks sternly to VALMOTH and they both simultaneous pick up their respective cudgels and continue to beat ORVILLE who whelps, screams and tries unsuccessfully to elude them.*)

ORVILLE: I'm a doctor! A specialist! A brain surgeon! A chiropractor! A chiropodist! I'm anything you say I am.

VALMOTH: Finally.

LUCIEN: You see—with a few good strokes, he admits to all the medical skills he possesses. Fascinating, isn't it?

VALMOTH: I'm delighted to find you reasonable, at last. This was really quite wearing me out.

ORVILLE: I'm so sorry.

LUCIEN: We're not as young as we were, you know. It's really quite cruel to make us exert ourselves like that.

ORVILLE: I'm sorry for the inconvenience, I assure you. It just went right out of my head. Of course, a doctor. How silly to have forgotten it.

VALMOTH: And I can tell you, you won't regret revealing your true identity to us. We'll make it worth your while.

ORVILLE: Now that that's all settled—maybe you could tell me, what sort of doctor I am? I mean—just to bring it all back into my mind.
LUCIEN: One of the most remarkable doctors in the entire world.
ORVILLE: Ah ha.
VALMOTH: One whose cures are virtually miraculous.
ORVILLE: Miraculous, you say.
LUCIEN: That woman from the hill who was practically dead and ready to be buried. You brought her round with a few drops of your own concoction and she won first prize at the Harvest Moon ball.
ORVILLE: She did?
VALMOTH: And that child who fell from the belfry and broke every bone in his body. What was that mixture you used to heal him in a moment, so he could cycle away to his baseball game?
ORVILLE: Ah the mixture. Well. Professional secret. Couldn't possibly divulge that—except to fellow doctors.—You're not by any chance…?
VALMOTH: Would it were so, Professor. But alas, we are ignorant laymen. But we'll take you to a house where your cures will be especially welcome and rewarded.
ORVILLE: Rewarded.
VALMOTH: You can ask any fee you like. There'll be no haggling about that.
ORVILLE: Any fee?
VALMOTH: Our client is extremely well off and will pay whatever you ask.
ORVILLE: *(Beat.)* I don't know how it could have slipped my mind—being a doctor I mean—but it's all back, it's all clear.
LUCIEN: Thank God.
ORVILLE: Well—where to?
VALMOTH: The manor is not far away. The patient is a beautiful young woman who, alas, has lost her speech.
ORVILLE: Quite understandable, isn't it? I mean. People are always losing things. You lost your temper. I lost my memory. She lost her speech.
VALMOTH: We'd better be off.
ORVILLE: But my doctor's gown. I'm afraid I've lost that as well.
VALMOTH: We'll get one on the way. No problem. It would be best if you looked official.
(ORVILLE solemnly presents his jug, which has suddenly become a sacred object, to VALMOTH.)
ORVILLE: Take hold of that. It's where I keep my secret potions. I'd be completely lost without it.
(VALMOTH gingerly and with great care takes the jug.)

LUCIEN: Isn't it heartwarming to see a great man restored to his senses and his true calling.
VALMOTH: If ever one doubted the existence of God, miracles like this would restore one's faith.
ORVILLE: Follow me gentlemen and lead the way.
(The three, with ORVILLE's jug held high, ceremoniously exit... MUSIC on their exit segues into Scene Two.)

SCENE TWO

Backdrop: A luxurious country manor in a gorgeous rustic setting. On stage, an embossed chair, an elegant chaise lounge and a few elegant furnishings. GERALDO, an affluent country squire, stands before LUCY-LYNN, his beautiful young daughter. He is conducting her in a speech therapy session.

GERALDO: *(Shaping his lips to emphasize the sound.)* Ahhhhhhhh...
(He gestures to LUCY-LYNN to repeat the sound. She opens her mouth to form the vowel sound but all that comes out is...)
LUCY-LYNN: Uhnnk.
GERALDO: *(Trying again.)* Eeeeeeeeeeeeee...
(He again gestures for her to repeat the sound but all that comes out is...)
LUCY-LYNN: Uhnnk.
GERALDO: *(Tries again.)* Ohhhhhhhhhhhhhh...
(Gestures for her to try again.)
LUCY-LYNN: Uhnnk.
(GERALDO, using his fingers, tries to shape her lips appropriately while she keeps "uhnnk"ing-out the same same sound—and he keeps repeating "Ahhhh — Eeeeeeee—Ohhhhh." This last turns into a scream of pain as LUCY-LYNN inadvertently bites GERALDO's thumb and he pulls it out and begins nursing the wound. Frustrated, he mops his brow, kisses her on the cheek and she exits mournfully—just as EVANGELINE, a governess with an outsize, enormous bosom enters. The two exchange looks.)
EVANGELINE: Listen, Mr. Geraldo: If you ask me, the best medicine for Lucy-Lynn would be a good match with someone she loves.
GERALDO: Nobody asked you.
EVANGELINE: No, but they should have.

GERALDO: You're hired to look after my little boy, not give advice to the lovelorn.

EVANGELINE: You're getting nowhere with all these treatments. These last few weeks, we've had more doctors in this house than a dog has fleas. Lucy-Lynn doesn't need any pills and potions. She just needs a husband.

GERALDO: That just goes to show how little you know, my dear Evangeline. She couldn't possibly cope with a husband in her present state. And when I suggested we proceed with the wedding to Horatio, she had an immediate relapse.

EVANGELINE: Because you were trying to marry her off to that scarecrow. He's enough to make *anyone* go deaf and dumb. Why don't you let her get off with Leopold whom she actually fancies. I bet he'd marry her right now—just as she is.

GERALDO: You know as little about marriage as you do about medicine. This Leopold-fellow hasn't got a pot to piss in.

EVANGELINE: His uncle is extremely wealthy and he might inherit it all.

GERALDO: You can't rely on legacies, my dear Evangeline. Wills are like women. They're always being changed at the last last minute. There's nothing like having a tidy fortune you can be sure of.

EVANGELINE: Don't you believe it's better to be happy than to be rich?

GERALDO: *(Beat.)* What a quaint idea.

EVANGELINE: Everybody's always going around these days asking "What's he worth?" "How much has he got?" As if you could measure a man by the size of his bank account.

GERALDO: And what better measure is there? Would you measure him by his height, the breadth of his paunch or the length of his inside leg? Tell me how many zeroes a man has in his bank book and I don't give a damn how many diplomas or certificates he's got on the wall.

EVANGELINE: "What profiteth a man if he gain the whole world and lose his own soul?"—do you know who said that?

GERALDO: Some pathetic bankrupt, I shouldn't wonder.

(As the music starts, The Maid moves to the Enunciator and reveals a placard which reads EVANGELINE and GERALDO: DUET: "LOVE IS WHAT THE DOCTOR ORDERED.")

EVANGELINE:
Love is what the doctor ordered.
Love is what annoints you.

Money's crass and money's sordid
It'll always disappoint you.
Give a man a million dollars
And his days are full of strife.
Give him one small taste of love
He'll be happy all his life.
Love's the only secret potion.
Love's the remedy.
Love's the root of all emotion
Just try it and you'll see.

GERALDO:
Money is the panacea.
And money brings you pleasure.
Accumulate your wealth, my dear
Then make love at your leisure.
Hearts and flowers may be pleasant
When you're in your teens.
But you'll live just like a peasant
If you live beyond your means.
Money is the magic bullet.
Money is the cure-all.
If a woman wants to feel secure.
Money is the great elixir.
Whatever's wrong, it's bound to fix 'er,
It's the only sure-fire cure.
(GERALDO repeats his verse in counterpoint as they sing and dance.)

EVANGELINE:
Love's the only secret potion.
Love's the remedy
Love's the root of all emotion
Just try it and you'll see.
Give a man a million dollars,
And his days are full of strife.
Give him just a little taste of love,
And he'll be happy all his life.

(VALMOTH and LUCIEN enter excitedly.)

VALMOTH: A memorable day, Geraldo. A day that will go down in history. We've brought you a quite remarkable physician.
LUCIEN: One of *the* most remarkable physicians in the whole world in fact.
VALMOTH: Who's effected some miraculous cures.
LUCIEN: Brought people back from the dead, practically.
VALMOTH: He's a little eccentric at times—like all great men—a little bizarre, perhaps.
LUCIEN: But when he puts his mind to it, quite extraordinary.
VALMOTH: People of the highest station have come to him for treatment.
LUCIEN: And they have always been cured.
GERALDO: Well don't just stand there, bring him in; bring him in.
   (VALMOTH exits.)
EVANGELINE: *(To LUCIEN.)* He'll be just as useless as all the others. The ones with the needles, the ointments, the monkey-glands, the pig-livers.
LUCIEN: Don't be so uppity, sweetheart. Your job is to tend the little one, not stick your nose where it doesn't belong. Which is where it usually is—most of the time!
GERALDO: Temper, temper, Lucien.
LUCIEN: *(Under his breath.)* No respect, no respect whatsoever.
   (EVANGELINE gives her husband the finger as ORVILLE enters wearing a very long white surgical gown, a head-mirror and stethascope. His lumberjack shoes jut out from the bottom of the gown.)
GERALDO: *(Taking his hand.)* I am delighted to make your acquaintance.
ORVILLE: *(Not taking his hand.)* No flesh-fusion after two in the afternoon.
GERALDO: I beg your pardon.
ORVILLE: It increases the incidence of germicidal copulation. —Hippocrates.
GERALDO: Hippocrates says that?
ORVILLE: Indubitably.
GERALDO: And where is that?
ORVILLE: In the chapter on Germicidal Copulation, volume four.
GERALDO: *(Withdrawing his hand.)* Sorry, I didn't know.
ORVILLE: Quite all right, doctor.
GERALDO: Doctor? I'm not a doctor.
ORVILLE: You neither?
   (GERALDO looks to VALMOTH for clarification.)
VALMOTH: *(Under.)* Part of his eccentricity—just ignore it.
LUCIEN: Occasionally he needs reminding. *(Mimes the beating to ORVILLE.)*
ORVILLE: Ah yes, sorry. You were saying—
GERALDO: I don't think I was saying anything.

ORVILLE: Far and away the best thing. Everytime one opens one's mouth, germicidal airwaves come shooting down the larynx. The safest thing would be to keep the lips sealed twelve hours a day or place a tiny piece of gauze between the upper and lower gums—with a two inch aperture through which food may be occasionally introduced.

GERALDO: A rather extreme measure, wouldn't you say?

ORVILLE: *(Sternly.)* It's the price we all must pay for good health, kind sir! Or would you rather fester and expire with your chops wide open?

(GERALDO looks again to VALMOTH for some help, but VALMOTH just nods away his concern.)

GERALDO: My daughter sir, has fallen into a strange illness.

ORVILLE: I am overjoyed, sir.

GERALDO: Overjoyed?

ORVILLE: That I can be of use to your daughter. I would go even farther and say that I am delighted to be of use to you and your entire family. People like myself breed on disease, so to speak. It's our meat and drink. And nothing gives us greater pleasure than walking into a contaminated atmosphere with our surgical cutlass firmly in hand to rout out the toxic enemies of good health.

(GERALDO looks again to VALMOTH.)

GERALDO: I'm very glad to hear it.

ORVILLE: As well you should be.

GERALDO: It's an honor having you.

ORVILLE: It usually is.—Now what is your daughter's name?

GERALDO: Lucy-Lynn.

ORVILLE: An excellent name for a patient. Lucy-Lynn— *(To himself.)* Insu-lin—Thora-zin—Streptomya-cin…

GERALDO: Shall I *bring*-her-in?

ORVILLE: *(After a take.)* That's always the best way. —I've tried treating patients over long distances, but the strain on the lungs is something awful.— *(Suddenly clocking EVANGELINE'S bosom.)*—And who is that lovely lady over there, may I ask?

GERALDO: Evangeline, the governess who attends to my little boy.

(GERALDO exits to fetch LUCY-LYNN.)

ORVILLE: A vision of delight, if I do say so myself. *(Approaching her.)* All my modest knowledge is at your disposal, my dear lady. If you'd like a private examination, please do not hesitate. I can always fit in extra patients at a moment's notice although I must say you seem to be *(Ogling her bosom.)* quite healthy and ro-*bust*.

LUCIEN: *(Protesting the intimacy.)* That is my wife, sir!
ORVILLE: *(Caught.)* Your wife?
LUCIEN: My wife, sir.
ORVILLE: I am delighted to make both your acquaintances. Overjoyed.
   (He vigorously shakes LUCIEN's hand and embraces EVANGELINE, flapping her leg into her hand, à la Harpo.)
EVANGELINE: *(Pushing it off.)* A little less effusion, doctor.
ORVILLE: Exactly what I always say. *(Finger in the air.)* "Less effusion—less contusion." It is one of Galen's soundest principles. I'm glad you agree. *(To LUCIEN.)* I compliment you on your good woman, sir. She has one of the most remarkable stirnums I've ever seen. It's a rare example of *mammalianus-projectilus* and nothing would give me more pleasure than to exhibit it to my students.
LUCIEN: My wife does not give exhibitions, doctor!!
ORVILLE: *(Under.)* As far as you know.
LUCIEN: I beg your pardon!
ORVILLE: No need we're all friends here, and I sincerely hope it will always remain that way. *(He shakes LUCIEN's hand firmly and once again lifts his leg into EVANGELINE'S hand, à la Harpo.)*
   (GERALDO returns with LUCY-LYNN in tow. She is wearing a thin, Laura Ashley-style floral dress.)
ORVILLE: Ah, the patient.
GERALDO: My daughter, doctor. I've been very distressed by her condition for some time now and pray to God you'll be able to effect a cure.
ORVILLE: A lovely specimen.
   (Everyone stands around mesmerized as ORVILLE circles the girl, touching the muscles of her back, her neck, her arms, her waist. The latter tickles her and she lets out a little giggle.)
GERALDO: You've made her laugh, doctor.
ORVILLE: A good sign. Anyone who can laugh at a doctor is obviously of sound mind.
   (He takes out his stethascope, is about to place it on her breast, becomes conscious of everyone peering at him, thinks better of it, put it down. Takes out a tongue depressor and suggests by opening his own mouth that the patient should open hers. She does so, he gingerly places the tongue depressor into her mouth. She bites down on it. He tries to remove it. He can't. He tries with two hands. He still can't. He mimes that he needs help from the others. VALMOTH and LUCIEN take hold of LUCY-LYNN and try to hold her rigid while ORVILLE, bracing his knee on her hip for leverage, tries to get the tongue depressor out of her mouth.

Eventually, he succeeds. All tumble away, ORVILLE into EVANGELINE's bosom. Enjoying the sensation, he tumbles a second time onto her chest. Now that the tongue depressor has been removed, he inspects it carefully, shakes it in front of his ear, wraps it in a handkerchief and places it in the pocket of his gown. The others are suitably impressed.)

ORVILLE: Are you in pain, my dear?

LUCY-LYNN: *(Pointing to her mouth, head and throat.)* Uhnnk, uhnnk.

ORVILLE: What was that?

LUCY-LYNN: Uhnnk, uhnnk.

ORVILLE: Are you saying Onk? onk?

LUCIEN: Uhnnk—uhnnk.

ORVILLE: Ahnnk—ahnnk??

GERALDO: I think she's saying "uhnnk" doctor, "uhnnk."

LUCIEN: It's more like uh-*nunnk*, uh-*nunnk*.

VALMOTH: Or enk-enk.

(Everyone trying to reproduce LUCY-LYNN's sound experiments with their version of it until everyone is "uhnnk-ing" and "enking" in unison.)

ORVILLE: Shaddup! Sounds like a goddam pig farm in here! *(Recovering his aplomb.)* We need a much more tranquil atmosphere for the patient.

GERALDO: What do you think, doctor? She was just struck dumb—from nothing, from nowhere. And no one's been able to figure out the cause. We've had to postpone the wedding ceremony. She was just about to be married, poor girl.

ORVILLE: Married?

GERALDO: Her husband-to-be wanted her to be cured before the marriage took place.

ORVILLE: A rash move on his part. I can think of many married men who would find the prospect of a dumb wife a blessing.

GERALDO: But what can you do, doctor, to restore her speech?

ORVILLE: First we must diagnose.

GERALDO: Diagnose what?

ORVILLE: Diagnose the nose, of course.—Then the ears, the throat, the eyes, the breasts.

GERALDO: The breasts?

ORVILLE: Many diseases of the eyes-nose-and-throat are often traced back to abnormalities in the breasts.

EVANGELINE: *(Skeptically.)* What kind of abnormalities?

ORVILLE: *(Demonstrating on Evangeline.)* Claustrophobic Cleavage, Undernourished Nipples, Uneven Booblyitis.

EVANGELINE: Never heard of any of those things.
ORVILLE: There are more things in discombobulated bosoms than are dreamt of in your philosophy, dear lady.—If you'd seen as many decomposing breasts as I have, you'd learn to be more vigilant. Tell me, does she complain of pains?
GERALDO: She doesn't complain of anything—she can't talk.
ORVILLE: *(Sagely.)* Ah, that would follow. —Does she go regularly to—you know… *(Mimes crapping.)*
GERALDO: I think so.
ORVILLE: Easily?
GERALDO: I can't say.
ORVILLE: Fluently? Copiously?
GERALDO: You'd have to ask her that.
ORVILLE: *(Turning to her.)* Yes, do you— *(Remembering her problem.)* Never mind.
(He begins to take her pulse with one hand while holding his watch in the other. Becomes terrified by what he doesn't hear. Begins to shake his watch vigorously. Then LUCY-LYNN's wrist then his watch again. Finally, it starts up.)
ORVILLE: Thank God! I thought this watch had packed up for good! *(Listens again.)* The pulse in your daughter's arm is an unmistakeable indication that your daughter…is dumb.
GERALDO: That's it exactly.
VALMOTH: He's got it in one.
LUCIEN: Amazing perspicacity.
GERALDO: Can you tell me why that's come about?
ORVILLE: This stems directly from the fact that she has—"lost the power of speech."
GERALDO: Yes, but what's the *cause* of her losing her power of speech?
ORVILLE: All the specialists in this field tend to agree that it is the result of—"an obstruction to the action of the tongue."
GERALDO: Yes, but what's *caused* this obstruction?
ORVILLE: Aristotle has written a long discourse on precisely that subject. You haven't read it by any chance?
GERALDO: No. Have you?
ORVILLE: What's that?
GERALDO: Aristotle's discourse.
ORVILLE: Oh many times. A great man, Aristotle. A great man. He came up to about here I'd say. *(Raises his hand to indicate height.)* On some days, he was even taller. One of those men who the more knowledge he acquired, the greater he became. His view was—this was many years ago mind you—he's

since been superceded by much greater men—*(Raises his hand to indicate their height.)*—that the obstruction was caused by certain humors, or as you might say tumors, which were of an unwholesome nature that came about because of vapors, or as you might say capers, which affected the diseased areas by means of taking these areas and, as it were, filling them full of disease.—Let's see if I can make this simpler—Uh, do you know Latin?

GERALDO: Not a word.

ORVILLE: Ah, well then. It's a matter of the Cabricias archi thurman, or catalmus, singulariter haec Musa—or as you might say, bonus, bona, bonum—epithalium—valium—impalium—golly-wogaylium.

GERALDO: *(Tortured.)* Oh if only I'd applied myself at university.

VALMOTH: Profound.

LUCIEN: Very deep stuff.

EVANGELINE: So deep you can't get to the bottom of it. Unless of course, there is no bottom.

LUCIEN: Everything has a bottom, silly.

EVANGELINE: Yes, your silly bottom being a case in point,

(LUCIEN brushes off EVANGELINE and turns his attention back to the Doctor.)

ORVILLE: Now these vapors as I say, or capers, it doesn't really matter what you call them—it's all a matter of semantics—by moving from the left side where the liver is, over to the right side where the epigastrum connects up with the epithelium, they automatically meet up with the low-hanging branches of the cerebral cortex, and when that happens of course, the diaphragm, if you happen to be wearing one, reacts to the nervous shock, and at that point the ventricles on the right side…you're following all this, aren't you?

GERALDO: I'm trying to.

ORVILLE: The ventricles, as I say, invaded by these vapors and misled by the movement of the liver, produces the diaphragmatic action which immediately affects the ossabundus, nequeys, potarnium quipsa milus. —And of course the inevitable result of that is that your daughter is struck dumb.

EVANGELINE: *(Under.)* What a load of balls.

LUCIEN: Respect! Respect, Evangeline! You can't hold a candle to the hem of this man's gown.

EVANGELINE: If I did he'd go up in smoke.

GERALDO: A very fascinating account, doctor—though there is just one thing that bothers me: the position of the liver and the heart. It would seem you've got them a little reversed. The heart is on the left side, and the liver on the right.

ORVILLE: That used to be the case, you're quite right, but modern medical science has made that entirely optional.

GERALDO: *(Beat—trying to figure it out.)* Ah, I see.

ORVILLE: But there's no reason in the world you should know that. It's not as if you're up to date on all the latest medical research. Even I get confused some time.

GERALDO: Right, but then what is your opinion?

ORVILLE: My opinion?

GERALDO: What do you think we should do?

ORVILLE: Do?

GERALDO: About my daughter.

ORVILLE: Ah your daughter, of course. My opinion, and of course this is only a matter *of* opinion—no doubt other specialists will have other opinions—but then, you've consulted me in this matter so I don't see why we should consider the opinions of all these other doctors, especially since they're not here—or are they?

GERALDO: No, no they're not.

ORVILLE: Well then, my opinion is we should put her to bed immediately and give her some bread soaked in wine.

GERALDO: *(Beat.)* And why is that?

ORVILLE: *Because* the mixture of bread and wine has, over the millenia, created a susceptibility on the part of people to talk. That's precisely what they give parrots you know, and they never have any trouble talking. Indeed, the problem with parrots is getting them to shut up!

GERALDO: *(Beat.)* That's true, of course, bread and wine, I had quite forgotten that. Brilliant, brilliant. Quick, bring some bread and wine.

ORVILLE: I'd say five slices of bread dipped in a litre of wine would do it. I'd better test the wine myself to make sure it's the right vintage. If it's a bad year, it will only impede the treatment.

GERALDO: Some wine for the doctor.

(Female Servants bring three stoups of wine; ORVILLE helps himself to two of them.)

ORVILLE: *(With wine bottles.)* I'll come back and supervise the treatment myself but I'll need all of you to assist.

GERALDO: How can I ever thank you?

ORVILLE: I'm sure if we both put our heads together we'll find a way.

GERALDO: May I kiss your hand.

ORVILLE: *(Looks at it for a moment.)* Why not?

(GERALDO kisses ORVILLE's hand. ORVILLE decides VALMOTH and

LUCIEN should do the same. He allows them each a peck; they bow and back out humbly as if to royalty. EVANGELINE, unimpressed, is also about to go when ORVILLE stops her.)

ORVILLE: Master Geraldo, I think it would be best to lay on some medication for your governess as well.

EVANGELINE: Me? There's nothing wrong with me.

ORVILLE: Of course not, but what is it that's invariably found at the onset of the worst kinds of illness? Nothing more nor less than good health! It never fails. Healthy today, expiring tomorrow. I think a little enema and massage are probably what's called for.

GERALDO: I don't understand. If the lady isn't sick…

ORVILLE: We drink to avoid thirst; we eat, to make sure we won't starve; we sleep to insure we'll be wakeful the next morning. We should always take medication when we're feeling well. That is the very essence of preventive medicine.

EVANGELINE: I don't wish to have anything alien put into my body, thank you.

ORVILLE: *(Curiously.)* Strange thing for a *woman* to say.

(EVANGELINE turns on her heel and leaves.)

GERALDO: *(Taking out checkbook.)* And now sir…

ORVILLE: Ey?

GERALDO: I want to pay you, doctor.

ORVILLE: Pay me?

GERALDO: To show my appreciation.

ORVILLE: I can't allow it, kind sir.

GERALDO: But your fee…

ORVILLE: By no means.

GERALDO: But I insist.

ORVILLE: It isn't right, kind sir.

GERALDO: Nonsense. *(Hands him check.)*

ORVILLE: I am not a mercenary man.

GERALDO: I quite see that.

ORVILLE: This goes against my grain, sir.

GERALDO: I quite understand.

ORVILLE: I seek no personal advantage.

GERALDO: Why should you?

ORVILLE: I serve a higher calling.

GERALDO: Don't we all.

ORVILLE: *(Quick glance.)* It's not signed.

GERALDO: Ah yes. *(Signs it.)*

(GERALDO holds out his hand. ORVILLE shakes it. GERALDO exits. Once out of sight, ORVILLE unfolds the check and looks at the stupendous amount. He reels for a moment at the size of the fee, rushes to the easel Stage Right and reveals the next Enunciator card which resads: ORVILLE: A MUSICAL SOLILOQUY.)

ORVILLE:
    See the cunning look upon my face
    Just like a sly piranna
    My Latin, I grant you, is a disgrace
    But like it or not, I've def'nitely got
    The hang of the bedside manner.

    I can diagnose in weighty prose
    Deliv'ring my prognosis;
    Tell 'em that they've got the clap
    Though they chew their cud
    And spit up blood,
    And die of tuberculosis.
    Medicate 'em and sedate 'em
    Through endless miseries
    Inoculate 'em, dehydrate 'em
    And if they bicker, they'll grow much sicker
    When they tote up all my fees.

    I am, I ween, a true M.D.
    O fortune and O fame.
    Not a single little letter
    Is found after my name.
    This GP's no PHD
    And yet I've hit a homer.
    Devoid of knowledge,
    No medical college,
    Not even a diploma!

    For if you spout the gibberish,
    It confidence instills,
    And when they're feeling liverish
    Just fill 'em up with pills.

Shove a needle up their ass
And give 'em tests galore.
Take their urine in a glass
Don't tell 'em what it's for.

I'll quietly pontificate
And tell them to be brave.
Sign 'em up and ship 'em out:
From perjury to surgery,
The Sick Bed to the Grave.

(On repeat of chorus, two Nurses in starched white uniforms appear. Instantly, their nurses' outfits transform into Spanish-dancer costumes, the wraparound skirts becoming wide, long and floral; their nurse's caps, combs and veils à L'Espagnole. One of them plunks a toreodor's hat on ORVILLE's head; the other, a bullfighter's cap around his shoulders. Thus caparisoned, the three perform a wild Spanish tango then the nurse-gypsies, gathering up all their costume bits, vanish as mysteriously as they appeared.)

CHORUS:
　　I am, I ween, a true M.D.
　　O Fortune and O fame
　　Not a single letter
　　Is found after my name
　　This GP's no PHD
　　But I will make this confession
　　By God, it's great
　　To be a member of
　　The medical profession.

(Kisses the check and puts it in his pocket and rushes to the Enunciator to display the next card which reads: LUCY-LYNN and LEOPOLD; LOVE DUET. Lyrical and romantic music, as LEOPOLD leaps on from Stage Right and LUCY-LYNN from the left. After checking that no one is about, they turn lovingly to one another.)

LUCY-LYNN:　My Leopold.
LEOPOLD:　　My Lucy-Lynn.

(Crashing romantic music as the two lovers sweep into each other's arms, passionately embrace and begin their duet.)

LUCY-LYNN: O misery, to be so cruelly parted!
LEOPOLD: O agony, to be so broken-hearted.
LUCY-LYNN: To pine for love of thee,
LEOPOLD: Excruti-ating-ly!
LUCY-LYNN: *(Madly.)* O this love's a torture for us both.
LEOPOLD: *(Resolutely.)* Not if we resolve to pledge our troth.

(Ardently, they adopt traditional lover's postures and pledge their love to one another.)

LEOPOLD: I'll cherish you in sickness and cherish you in health.
I'll cherish you in poverty, I'll cherish you in wealth.
LUCY: But will you promise faithfully to love but me alone?
LEOPOLD: How can a burning love expire?
LUCY: Ah well, it has been known.
LEOPOLD: It is you and you alone that I worship and adore.
LUCY: Does that mean you'll never look at others anymore?
LEOPOLD: My passion is a hurricane that nothing can restrain.
LUCY: And yet they say, there comes that day when strongest feelings wane.
BOTH: True love—strong-as-glue love, nothing-can-undo love,
Is what we're pledging.
Deep love, troubled-sleep love, wail-and-weep love
A love that knows no hedging.
And nothing in the world will ever sunder that strong link.
It will last forever and ever and ever—and ever—
(BEAT.) I think.
LEOPOLD: Our love is high and noble and can never be degraded.
LUCY: I'm sure of it my darling, though my daddy's not persuaded.
LEOPOLD: But parents don't decide these things; it's up to you and me.
LUCY: If that's the case our love is bound to be a fait-accompli.
LEOPOLD: I need to know your love is sure and never will it waver.
LUCY: But you might change, grow passing strange, and seek another flavor.
LEOPOLD: I swear by all the gods above and all the gods below!
LUCY: I love the way you say that. Well now, I guess we know.

BOTH:
> True love—strong-as-glue love, nothing-can-undo love,
> Is what we're pledging.
> Deep love, troubled-sleep love, wail-and-weep love
> A love that knows no hedging.
> And nothing in the world will ever sunder that strong link.
> It will last forever and ever and ever—and ever—
> *(BEAT.)* I think.

(They kiss—they part—they kiss again—they are about to reaffirm their love; they hesitate—they blow a kiss to one another. LUCY-LYNN goes. LEOPOLD stands fond, then uncertain, simultaneously amorous and confused. Hearing ORVILLE'S return, he conceals himself.
ORVILLE has finished one of the wine bottles and is working on the second. LEOPOLD reveals himself.)

LEOPOLD: I was hoping I'd catch you alone. I desperately need your help.

ORVILLE: *(Taking his wrist.)* Very soft pulse. Do you have a heart murmur?

LEOPOLD: I'm not ill sir. Or at least not in the usual sense. I do have a problem of the heart.

ORVILLE: I thought as much. I'm getting so good at this, I astound myself.

LEOPOLD: The thing is: my name is Leopold and I'm madly in love with Lucy-Lynn, the girl you just examined. And she's madly in love with me. —I think.—Her father is dead set against our getting together and so I hoped you might be able to help me out. I have a little plan worked out, but I need your help in order to make it work. *(Screaming into the stethascope which is on ORVILLEs ears.)* My entire happiness is at stake.

ORVILLE: *(Reacting to the deafening noise in his ears.)* What do you take me for? Would you compromise the dignity of a great physician by embroiling him in some sordid little affair-of-the-heart!?

LEOPOLD: Not so loud, they'll hear you.

ORVILLE: I'll make as much noise as I like. What impertinence!

LEOPOLD: Please calm down.

ORVILLE: A young Lothario comes to me to help him carry off a woman *and* a patient. Leaving me open to charges of professional misconduct! A malpractice suit perhaps.

LEOPOLD: But if you'd…

ORVILLE: It is the height of arrogance…the depth of depravity…an insult to end all insults…to put such a proposal to a man like me who…*(LEOPOLD, holding a wad of bills, presses half the wad into his hands.)*—I'm not referring to you, of course, I can see you're a regular sort of fellow with a good head on his shoulders, but there are some people around here who seem to believe that integrity has gone right out the window and there are no depths to which one would not sink. Oh that kind of thing just makes my blood boil.

LEOPOLD: I hope you don't mind my taking the liberty…

ORVILLE: Not at all. What are liberties for, if not to be taken. (God knows I've taken a few of my own this afternoon.) Now what can I do for you, my good man? *(Relieving LEOPOLD of the remaining wad of bills in his hand.)*

LEOPOLD: This is how it is. Lucy-Lynn's illness that you've been called in to cure, is completely made up. Her father has brought in dozens of specialists and therapists from every part of the country—and even abroad. Some have said it comes from the brain; others from the intestines or the spleen, the liver or the blood. But the fact is, the real cause is simply love. Lucy-Lynn has invented this condition in order to avoid a horrific marriage with a man her father is forcing on her.

ORVILLE: I already have great sympathy for your problem, young Leopold—even though I've only known you for a few moments. And you're obviously a man who knows exactly how to express himself. *(Quickly counting the wad of bills.)* The patient will either perish or be yours, or I'm no doctor. But first I must attend to her treatment. Wait for me in the garden and we'll consult together.

(LEOPOLD, checking fore and aft, tiptoes away.)

(As mechanistic music accompanying the following scene begins, the Enunciator card is changed to read: LUCY-LYNN GETS THE TREATMENT.

LUCIEN, VALMOTH, GERALDO wearing white surgical gloves, march out military-fashion and stand as on an assembly line. LUCY-LYNN at the end of the line, beside her ORVILLE who is supervising the procedure.

LUCIEN with wine bottle pours it into the glass held by VALMOTH who then passes it to GERALDO who dunks bread into wine and passes both to ORVILLE who feeds LUCY-LYNN bread and then, with one swig, empties the wineglass.

The empty wineglass is then passed back to GERALDO who passes it down the line to LUCIEN who refills it. VALMOTH now with a new piece of bread, begins the assembly-line process all over again. It ends as before with ORVILLE feeding the bread to LUCY-LYNN and then emptying the wineglass in one swig and passing it back down the line.

This identical procedure is followed six times—getting progressively faster, ORVILLE progressively soused and LUCY-LYNN progressively more bloated.

When the bottle is empty, ORVILLE gives a signal, GERALDO, VAL-MOTH, and LUCIEN do an about-face and march off Stage Left. ORVILLE wobbles off after them and LUCY-LYNN, ready to barf, rushes off Stage Right. Blackout. Musical bridge.)

SCENE THREE

LEOPOLD now rigged up in a white medical gown similar to ORVILLE's is trying to get used to the costume. ORVILLE enters and adds a surgical mask to it that hangs down on LEOPOLD's chest.

ORVILLE: Perfect. You look just like an Interne. Just stick close and keep giving me those doe-eyed looks, and anything I say, just agree with it.
LEOPOLD: But I don't have any of the lingo. Could you give me a few medical terms to throw around?
ORVILLE: Not necessary. All you need is the uniform and an inscrutable professional air.
LEOPOLD: What's that?
ORVILLE: Something like this. *(He puts it on.)* Now you try it.
(LEOPOLD tries it on).
ORVILLE: Not inscrutable enough.—Try again.
(LEOPOLD tries again.)
ORVILLE: It's not grave enough. If a doctor doesn't look grave, patients think he's frivolous. They see him in terms of golf courses and Mediterranean cruises instead of consulting rooms and operating theatres. Now let's say they ask you for a medical opinion, what do you say?
LEOPOLD: *(About to pontificate, realizes he hasn't got the words.)* What *do* I say?
ORVILLE: You say: "It may be quite serious. It might need surgery. The chances of success are 50-50. It might take a year to heal up. No one can give any guarantees." Or contrariwise: "It may be nothing at all. A little medication and it will all clear up. Just have a lot of rest and eat regularly." Of course the ideal diagnosis tries to combine a little of each. "It's quite serious. It may be nothing at all. It might need major surgery; on the other hand it might clear up by itself. If it doesn't heal in a month, it may take a year."

LEOPOLD: But what does all that mean?

ORVILLE: Nothing, of course. But you've left all your options open. If the patient dies, you predicted it. If he gets well, you said as much. If he gets well and *then* he dies, you got them coming and going. Either way, you get paid. If a tailor cuts your suit all wrong, you cancel the order and he's out of pocket. If the shoemaker ruins your shoes, he's got to pay for the damage. But in our job, we can screw up by the numbers and it never costs us a penny. Diagnosis-Second Opinion-New diagnosis-Third opinion—etc. etc. and so on. If you're lucky you can keep it going forever—or until the patient passes away. And when that happens, it's never your fault. It's always the patient's fault. Operation was a success; the patient died. Who's to blame? The patient, of course. Have you ever heard of a dead man complaining he was killed by his doctor?

LEOPOLD: Now that you mention it…

ORVILLE: When I think of all those goddam years I spent chopping wood…
(Notices EVANGELINE.) Ah this is one of my would-be patients. Make yourself scarce for awhile, will you?
(LEOPOLD nips away as EVANGELINE enters.)

ORVILLE: Ah, my Vision of Delight, back again. Just the sight of you purges all the melancholia from my soul.

EVANGELINE: They say there's nothing like a nice purge now and again.

ORVILLE: I almost wish you *would* fall ill so that I could use all the skill at my command to restore you to spanking good health.

EVANGELINE: That's a little perverse, doctor.

ORVILLE: A little perversity always adds a touch of spice to a relationship, don't you think?

EVANGELINE: I couldn't say doctor. I don't have any relationships; I'm a *married* woman.

ORVILLE: And to such a sour, grouchy, jealous husband.

EVANGELINE: We all play the hand we're dealt.

ORVILLE: But with such a man, the deck is stacked against you, dear Evangeline. A man who watches you like a hawk; who won't let you mix with strangers.

EVANGELINE: And that's not even the half of it, doctor.

ORVILLE: Oh when I think how you're mistreated, it makes my blood boil. There are some people I could name, people very close at hand in fact, who would treat you with the sweet and loving tenderness that you deserve. Who would *(Honing into her bosom.)* appreciate all your finer points. The "pinnacles" of your sweet nature and firm, outstanding, one might almost say protruding, virtues. *(He butches down his randiness and diverts.)* How could such a lovely

and innocent creature stoop to such a crass, gauche, stupid—I apologize for insulting your good husband…
EVANGELINE: No need. He's everything you say he is.
ORVILLE: He is?
EVANGELINE: I'm afraid he is.

(The music begins and the Enunciator card now reads: ORVILLE and EVANGELINE; SEDUCTION NUMBER.)

ORVILLE:
    You know what Plato used to say,
    (All things he comprehended.)
    A woman needs to have the man
    For whom she was intended.
    A Juliet needs a Romeo;
    A Pyramus a Thisbe.
    A man who finds his proper gal
    That gal, you'll see, will his be.

CHORUS:
    There's something in your way of walking
    There's something in your laugh,
    That says to me you're meant to be
    My better half.

    There's something in your manner
    The chatter in your chat,
    That says to me that you are meant to be
    My pussycat.
    So let's not try to fight it sweetie
    It's there for all to see
    That potent drug, the mighty tug
    Of Destiny.

EVANGELINE:
    Now Aristotle says somewhere
    (Or maybe it was Proust)
    That any man who wants to get
    A proper girl seduced

> Just needs to throw a little line
> To flatter and persuade her
> And in a trice, she's in his vice
> And finds that he's waylaid her.

CHORUS:
> There's something in your way of talking
> The way you cock your head
> That says you're trying hard to get
> Me into bed.
>
> There's something in your manner
> I cannot say just what
> But I surmise from those big eyes this guy is
> Hot to trot.
> I think we better cool it, doctor
> And look before we leap
> I like my bed uninhabited
> When I climb inside to sleep.

ORVILLE: There something in your way of walking
Something in your laugh
EVANGELINE: Don't push your luck
You'll come unstuck
TOGETHER: You're not my better half.
I'll be your better half.

(ORVILLE made even hotter by the song-and-dance comes in for the kill with EVANGELINE. LUCIEN, unseen by both, saunters quietly into the scene from behind.)

ORVILLE: I hate to say it but truth is truth, your husband's the sort of man that almost cries out to be cuckolded by a sweet, charming and selfless wife—as a *punishment* against his rude, crude, jealous behavior. Why no one would blame you if you gave yourself—brazenly helplessly (and frequently)—to another man who could truly appreciate your *(Drooling over EVANGELINE's bosom.)*...your...your... *(Sees LUCIEN looming behind.)* You're quite right to consult me about those pains. I suggest an ointment of goat's milk and

112 • MOLIÈRE

lime juice, vigorously rubbed on your chest twice a day and once before retiring. Come along, I'll show you how to apply it.

(EVANGELINE, sashays out with ORVILLE in tow. GERALDO enters from the opposite side.)

GERALDO: Have you seen the Doctor around?

LUCIEN: *(Seething to himself.)* He's, as you might say, hard by.

GERALDO: Hard by?

LUCIEN: *Very* hard by—and the sooner I see him in hell the happier I'll be.

GERALDO: See if you can find my daughter, will you?

(LUCIEN snorting and simmering, stomps out. As ORVILLE and LEOPOLD enter from the other side. LEOPOLD now wears his surgical mask.)

GERALDO: Ah, doctor, I was just asking for you.

ORVILLE: I was just outside, getting my rocks off.

GERALDO: I beg your pardon!

ORVILLE: *(Holding them up in his hand.)* My healing stones from the Temples of Tibet. Someone seems to have piled them on the front lawn and I was just getting them off— How does our patient?

GERALDO: She took a turn for the worse after the medication.

ORVILLE: Perfect—that means it's working.

GERALDO: She's looking rather the worse for wear, doctor.

ORVILLE: Good. Patients shouldn't glow with health. It only dilutes the power of the medicine and makes it hard to recognize the improvement when it appears.

GERALDO: *(Nudging him regarding LEOPOLD.)* Who is…um…?

ORVILLE: Ah, my anesthesiologist?

GERALDO: *(Alarmed.)* Is surgery going to be necessary, do you think?

ORVILLE: One can never say, but one should be prepared for anything. I remember once I had to operate in the middle of the Mojave desert armed only with a screw driver and a pair of nail clippers. It was a challenge, but it's amazing how pressure brings out the best in a man.

(GERALDO hesitatingly offers his hand to LEOPOLD who takes it then has his hand sanitized by ORVILLE with a small antiseptic spray. LUCY-LYNN enters, registers surprize to discover LEOPOLD, who quickly whips his surgical mask off and then on again to reveal himself.)

ORVILLE: Ah, the patient. How are we today?

LUCY-LYNN: Uhnnk.

ORVILLE: Good, her condition is stable. *(To LEOPOLD.)* Give her a brief pre-operative examination just in case it comes to it, will you?

(LEOPOLD draws LUCY-LYNN aside as GERALDO tries to see what precisely

the anesthesiologist is doing with his daughter. During the speech, ORVILLE puts his arm around GERALDO's shoulder and under his chin, in various attempts to distract him from LEOPOLD.)

ORVILLE: *(Walking him around.)* It's always been a matter of great dispute as to whose health was more vulnerable, the man or the woman's. My own feeling is, *(Turning GERALDO's head away from the lovers.)*—I hope you're taking all this in, Mr. Geraldo. —My own feeling has always been *the woman's*. Since most diseases are contracted from germs or deadly vapours in the air and most women talk much more than men, their mouths, being constantly open, invite contagion into the system much more readily. *(Again steering GERALDO away from the lovers.)* Now to prove this theory, we took two women—put a gauze over one woman's mouth and let the other one jabber away quite freely. *(Turning his head away from the lovers.)* Well as you might suspect, the jabbering woman came down with innumerable maladies including asthma, gout and dropsy, and surprisingly enough, the woman with the gauze over her mouth, because it was inadvertently tied too tight, developed a breathing disability and expired before the experiment was concluded—leaving the whole question still up in the air.

(Throughout the previous scene, LEOPOLD continually whispers soft nothings into LUCY-LYNN's ears, gradually stirring her amorous instincts and ultimately causing her to erupt.)

LUCY-LYNN: It's no use, it's no use, IT'S NO USE!!! Nothing will ever make me do it!

(GERALDO hearing his daughter's voice, wheels toward her.)

GERALDO: My daughter! She's speaking, she's speaking! *(Turns and kisses ORVILLE.)* How can I ever thank you, you marvellous, marvellous doctor! Name your fee! It's yours, whatever is!

ORVILLE: *(Wiping his brow.)* One of the toughest cases I've ever had!

LUCY-LYNN: *(Who is now revealed to have a broad Valley-girl accent)* Yes I've recovered my speech—but only to tell you that I will never marry any other man but Leopold. There's no point in pushing Horatio or anyone else on to me.

GERALDO: But—

LUCY-LYNN: Nothing will ever change my mind!

GERALDO: What—

LUCY-LYNN: Nothing you say will do any good!

GERALDO: I—

LUCY-LYNN: My mind's made up and nothing will change it!

GERALDO: But—

LUCY-LYNN: There's no power on earth that will make me give him up!

GERALDO: I've…
LUCY-LYNN: You can do what you like!
GERALDO: He…
LUCY-LYNN: Disown me, beat me, lock me up!
GERALDO: But I—
LUCY-LYNN: It doesn't matter what.
GERALDO: If I—
LUCY-LYNN: I'd rather become a nun than marry someone I can't bear.
GERALDO: But—
LUCY-LYNN: No, no, no!! I won't do it. I'll *never* do it! You can't make me do it! And that's that!!
GERALDO: *(To ORVILLE.)* Do you think you could make her dumb again?!
ORVILLE: Can't do that— *(Holding up knee hammer.)* but I could make you deaf, if you like.
GERALDO: So my sprightly little girl, you think you can—
LUCY-LYNN: It's absolutely useless. Save your breath!
GERALDO: Not only will you marry Horatio—you'll marry him this very day.
LUCY-LYNN: He'll be a widow by tomorrow because I'll kill myself tonight.
ORVILLE: Mr. Geraldo, your daughter is not yet completely recovered. May I be allowed to medicate matters.
GERALDO: I think she needs locking up in a madhouse, if you ask me.
ORVILLE: We have to cure both the mind and the body; sometimes both at once. *(To LEOPOLD, issuing instructions.)* As you see, the girl's father is opposed to this match and so something has to be done double-quick. Her tempertaure is rising very fast and unless it gets stabilized, there's no telling what will happen. As I see it, the only real cure is a dose of Lam-out-while-you-can combined with two drams of matrimonium and a tablespoon of preacheritis. She may object to this treatment but you're an old hand at these kinds of cases and I'm sure you'll be able to persuade her to swallow her medicine. Now I suggest you deal patiently with the patient but don't lose any time, while I explain the prognosis to the girl's father. Don't dally. You know this kind of remedy always works best if administered quickly.
(LEOPOLD grabs LUCY-LYNN and wheels her out.)
GERALDO: Did you ever see such insolence?
ORVILLE: Women today! I don't know what things are coming to.
GERALDO: Wanting to go off with that useless twerp Leopold when I've managed to get her a first-class man with a first-class fortune.
ORVILLE: *(Blandly pontificating.)* Men are led by their noses—women by their genitals.

GERALDO: Ey?

ORVILLE: *(Caught, turns it into a quote.)* Um, Karen Horney!

GERALDO: As soon as I learned of her fatal weakness, I kept that fortune hunter as far away from her as possible.

ORVILLE: Smart move.

GERALDO: I tore up all his letters. Stopped all communication.

ORVILLE: Sensible.

GERALDO: If they'd have got together, who knows what would have happened. A hot-blooded man—an impressionable girl!

ORVILLE: Ughhh, sickening.

GERALDO: She'd have run him off with him just like that. She's capable of it.

ORVILLE: *(Nauseous.)* Sex, sex, sex.

GERALDO: I know he's tried to get in to see her a dozen times.

ORVILLE: Licentious beast.

GERALDO: But he didn't count on a clever father with a will of iron.

ORVILLE: Bully for you!

GERALDO: I'll keep him in his place, all right.

ORVILLE: Have to get up early in the morning.

GERALDO: Why?

ORVILLE: To get the jump on you.

GERALDO: You can say that again!

(LUCIEN and VALMOTH enter. Breathing in unison.)

LUCIEN: Geraldo, she's gone. Taken off with that…that…doctor.

GERALDO: *(Breathing in unison with them.)* What!? My daughter?! —The doctor!??

VALMOTH: *(Breathing.)* It was that Leopold-fellow—in disguise.

GERALDO: *(Stops the unison breathing. VALMOTH and LUCIEN stop simultaneously.)* Leopold!!! —Stop him, stop him!!

VALMOTH: It's too late. They're getting married.

LUCIEN: *(Pointing to ORVILLE.)* It's him. It's all his doing! He put him up to it.
(Ominously, all bear down on ORVILLE. GERALDO twisting the stethascope around his neck like a noose.)

GERALDO: I'll get you for this. It'll take more than ten doctors to put you together again. *(Dashes out and runs smack into MARTI.)*

MARTI: Excuse me, could you tell me where…

GERALDO: Get out of my way! *(Almost knocks her down. Exits.)*

MARTI: That's not very nice. I've had a lot of trouble finding this house and now… *(Runs into EVANGELINE.)* I wonder if you can help me, I'm looking for someone who's passing himself off as a doctor.

EVANGELINE: A short fellow in a white coat who talks a good game but can't quite cut the mustard.

MARTI: That's right. How did *you* know? *(EVANGELINE dryly points her finger in ORVILLE's direction where she encounters LUCIEN and VALMOTH.)* Ah, there you are. Can you tell me what happened to that doctor I recommended to you?

VALMOTH: Oh you mean the special specialist with the great powers of healing?

MARTI: That's right.

BOTH: There he is! *(Pointing to where ORVILLE was, but is no longer as he has tiptoed upstage and become an extension of the sculpture.)*

BOTH: There he is! *(Pointing to where he is standing, trying to make himself inconspicuous.)*

LUCIEN: Take a good look. He's going to be strung up in a matter of hours. — He'll be well and truly hung.

MARTI: *(Under.)* That'd be a first.

LUCIEN: Ey?

MARTI: Him being well hung. Are you sure we're talking about the same feller.

LUCIEN: Thin, weedy, horny; head like an artichoke, body like a bent thistle.

MARTI: That's him. What's he charged with?

VALMOTH: Kidnapping,

LUCIEN: Larceny!

VALMOTH: Fraud!

LUCIEN: *(Looking to EVANGELINE.)*…and probably rape.

MARTI: Orville, is all of this true?

ORVILLE: There's lots of mitigating circumstances.

MARTI: Like what?

ORVILLE: I haven't made them up yet.

MARTI: If you'd stuck to the woodcutting, none of this would've happened.

ORVILLE: *(To BIG ROB.)* What're *you* doing here?

BIG ROB: Marti brung me.

(ORVILLE looks accusingly at MARTI.)

MARTI: I needed a drill—you were gone—so I borrowed his tool.

ORVILLE: *(Irate.)* Will you just get out'a here.

MARTI: Not if you're going to be hung. I wouldn't miss that for anything.

(GERALDO, pushes through MARTI and BIG ROB, re-entering.)

GERALDO: The police will be here any minute. Given the size of all your crimes, you can expect thirty years to life.

ORVILLE: Could we work out a plea bargain?
GERALDO: What kind've plea bargain?
ORVILLE: You drop all the charges and I won't tell anybody about how you got duped by Leopold.
(GERALDO pulls back to take a whallop at ORVILLE and just at that moment, LEOPOLD and LUCY-LYNN wearing trapeze costumes and capes, enter and wedge themselves between GERALDO's fist and ORVILLE.)
LEOPOLD: Mr. Geraldo. *(Gulps.)*—Father—I've come back to return Lucy-Lynn to you. We were going to get married and join a travelling circus as trapeze artists but, as Lucy gets airsick and I suffer from vertigo, we decided that would be a silly thing to do. Besides, I don't want to steal your daughter out from under you. I'd rather you gave her to me of your own free will.
(GERALDO, unmoved, winds up to deliver another whallop, but LEOPOLD quickly intercedes.)
LEOPOLD: And there is one other bit of information I have to convey: I've just learned that my uncle, who owned six oil wells and four gold mines, has died and left me his entire fortune.
GERALDO: *(Beat—GERALDO unwinds the fist with which he was going to take a whallop at LEOPOLD and places it around his shoulder.)* Leopold, now that I look at you closely, I seem to see you in a completely new light. Any man that can sneak into my house, pretend to be a doctor, steal my daughter, elope with her, play me for a fool and then come back to make amends—can't be all bad. I give you my daughter's hand with a full and joyous heart.
LUCY-LYNN: *(Affectionately).* Oh Daddy, I knew you weren't as big a bastard as everyone said.
(GERALDO, LEOPOLD and LUCY-LYNN share improvised expressions of gratitude and forgiveness.)
ORVILLE: Since everyone seems to be getting a reprieve, Mr. Geraldo, I wonder if…
GERALDO: *(Vindictively.)* You are a scoundrel, a charlatan and an insufferable phoney of the first water!
ORVILLE: But I did help you to get a wealthy son-in-law!
GERALDO: That's true. *(ORVILLE, anticipating forgiveness, firmly extends his hand.)* We'll see if we can get you a little time off for good behavior. *(ORVILLE's handshake wilts in mid-air.)*
MARTI: And you never would have become such an honored doctor, if it wasn't for me.
ORVILLE: Or got beaten black and blue.
MARTI: What's a few bruises between a really loving couple.

ORVILLE: I don't know. If I ever meet one, I'll ask 'em.

(As the music begins to swell behind them and the company forms in the front of the stage, the Maid places the last Enunciator sign on the easel which reads: THE BIG FINISH. FULL COMPANY.)

FINALE:
>Love's the only secret potion,
>Love's the remedy.
>Love's the root of all emotion
>Just try it and you'll see.
>Give a man a million dollars,
>And his days are full of strife.
>Give him just a little taste of love,
>And he'll be happy all his life.

GERALDO:
>I thought money ruled the world,
>Now I see it just upsets it.
>Cash crucifies and besides,
>The taxman always gets it!

LEOPOLD:
>I fell in love with Lucy-Lynn
>Without a pot to piss in.
>But love just sucks without big bucks,
>What a sweet transition!

LUCY-LYNN:
>Now Leopold is in the dough,
>The wedding'll be divine.
>And if he splits, and calls it quits,
>The alimony's mine!

ALL:
>Now we all have what we're wanting,
>And it's so delightful.
>Everything was rather daunting
>And the prospects frightful.

> Love has changed our whole prognosis
> Everything is clear and bright.
> The garden's full of roses,
> Not a single weed in sight.
> Now we will retire.
> Nothin' more to do now,
> Love has banished all our cares and strife.
> Give a man a gal to sing to,
> A pair of lovin' arms to cling to,
> And he'll be happy all his life.

MARTI:
> I never fancied doctors' ways
> Nothing was absurder.
> They'd ask me to strip—I'd cry: "Pip pip!"
> Then they'd never take it further.

EVANGELINE:
> I thought "I do" meant I mustn't screw
> That love-affairs were vices.
> But they're the icing on the cake,
> 'N' I've got a thousand slices.

ORVILLE:
> Now that I'm a doctor-true,
> In my clinic I'll carouse.
> "All Ladies Free," if they'll treat me,
> And babies are on the house.

WOMEN: *(Singing in counterpoint with men.)*
> Love's the only secret potion,
> Love's the remedy.
> Love's the root of all emotion
> Just try it and you'll see.
> Give a man a million dollars,
> And his days are full of strife.
> Give him just a little taste of love,
> And he'll be happy all his life.

MEN: *(Counterpoint to the former.)*
>Now we all have what we're wanting,
>And it's so delightful.
>Everything was rather daunting
>And the prospects frightful.
>Love has changed our whole prognosis
>Everything is clear and bright.
>The garden's full of roses,
>Not a single weed in sight.
>Now we will retire.
>Nothin' more to do now,
>Love has banished all our cares and strife.
>Give a man a gal to sing to,
>A pair of lovin' arms to cling to,
>And he'll be happy all his life.

(Curtain.)

END OF PLAY

Smith and Kraus *Books for Actors*
GREAT TRANSLATIONS FOR ACTORS SERIES

Anthologies and Collections
    Chekhov: Four Plays, tr. by Carol Rocamora
    Chekhov's Vaudevilles, tr. by Carol Rocamora
    Ibsen: Four Major Plays, tr. by R. Davis & B. Johnston
    Ibsen Volume II: Four Plays, tr. by Brian Johnston
    Ibsen Volume III: Four Plays, tr. by Brian Johnston
    Marivaux: Three Plays, tr. by Stephen Wadsworth
    Arthur Schnitzler: Four Major Plays, tr. by Carl Mueller
    Villeggiatura: The Trilogy by Carlo Goldoni, tr. by Robert Cornthwaite

Classics
    The Coffee Shop by Carlo Goldoni, tr. by Robert Cornthwaite
    Cyrano de Bergerac by Edmond Rostand, tr. by Charles Marowitz
    Emperor and Galilean by Henrik Ibsen, tr. by Brian Johnston
    A Glass of Water by Eugene Scribe, tr. by Robert Cornthwaite
    Mercadet by Honoré de Balzac, tr. by Robert Cornthwaite
    The Sea Gull by Anton Chekhov, tr. by N. Saunders & F. Dwyer
    Spite for Spite by Agustin Moreto, tr. by Dakin Matthews
    The Summer People by Maxim Gorky, tr. by N. Saunders & F. Dwyer
    Three Sisters by Anton Chekhov, tr. by Lanford Wilson
    The Wood Demon by Anton Chekhov, tr. by N. Saunders & F. Dwyer
    Zoyka's Apartment by Mikhail Bulgakov, tr. by N. Saunders & F. Dwyer

If you require prepublication information about upcoming Smith and Kraus books, you may receive our semiannual catalogue, free of charge, by sending your name and address to *Smith and Kraus Catalogue, P.O. Box 127, Lyme, NH 03768. Or call us at (603) 643-6431, fax (603) 922-3348. www.SmithKraus.Com*